Risk Management Today

A How-to Guide for Local Government

Edited by
Natalie Wasserman
Dean G. Phelus

prima

ICMA

Published in cooperation with the
Public Risk and Insurance Management Association by the
International City Management Association

PRACTICAL MANAGEMENT SERIES
Barbara H. Moore, Editor

Risk Management Today
Capital Financing Strategies for Local Governments
Creative Personnel Practices
The Entrepreneur in Local Government
Human Services on a Limited Budget
Microcomputers in Local Government
Police Management Today
Practical Financial Management
Shaping the Local Economy
Successful Negotiating in Local Government
Telecommunications for Local Government

The Practical Management Series is devoted to the presentation of information and ideas from diverse sources. The views expressed in this book are those of the contributors and are not necessarily those of the International City Management Association or the Public Risk and Insurance Management Association.

Library of Congress Cataloging-in-Publication Data
Main entry under title:
Risk management today.
(Practical management series)
1. Insurance, Government risks—Management.
2. Government liability. 3. Local government.
I. Wasserman, Natalie. II. Phelus, Dean G. III. Public
Risk and Insurance Management Association (U.S.)
IV. International City Management Association.
V. Series.
HG8207.R57 1985 352 85-19690
ISBN 0-87326-046-5

Printed in the United States of America.
91908988878685
54321

Foreword

Management of risk has reached crisis proportions in local government. Many cities and counties have found premiums skyrocketing, policies unexpectedly canceled, and insurance suddenly unavailable. They are fearful of increasing liability but unable to obtain or afford the coverage they seek.

Risk Management Today provides help for local governments as they grapple with these problems. It presents sound information and ideas on organizing for risk management; financing risk intelligently; dealing with such special areas of risk as public officials liability, police liability, and environmental impairment liability; and promoting risk control and safety in the workplace.

This book has been prepared jointly by the International City Management Association (ICMA) and the Public Risk and Insurance Management Association (PRIMA). These two organizations have worked closely since PRIMA was formed in 1978, and this mutual effort represents the commitment of both associations to help local governments during this critical period.

Risk Management Today is part of ICMA's continuing Practical Management Series, which is devoted to serving the needs of local government managers, department heads, and students for timely information on current issues and problems.

We wish to thank the organizations and individuals who granted permission to reprint their materials, and to the ICMA and PRIMA staff members who organized, compiled, and edited the volume. Thanks also go to David S. Arnold of the ICMA staff, who was of great help in planning the entire Practical Management Series.

William H. Hansell, Jr.
Executive Director
International City Management Association

Natalie Wasserman
Executive Director
Public Risk and Insurance Management Association

Risk Management Today:
A How-to Guide for Local Government

The International City Management Association is the professional and educational organization for chief appointed management executives in local government. The purposes of ICMA are to strengthen the quality of local government through professional management and to develop and disseminate new approaches to management through training programs, information services, and publications.

Managers, carrying a wide range of titles, serve cities, towns, counties, and councils of governments in all parts of the United States and Canada. These managers serve at the direction of elected councils and governing boards. ICMA serves these managers and local governments through many programs that aim at improving the manager's professional competence and strengthening the quality of all local governments.

The International City Management Association was founded in 1914; adopted its City Management Code of Ethics in 1924; and established its Institute for Training in Municipal Administration in 1934. The Institute, in turn, provided the basis for the Municipal Management Series, generally termed the "ICMA Green Books."

ICMA's interests and activities include public management education; standards of ethics for members; the *Municipal Year Book* and other data services; urban research; and newsletters, a monthly magazine, *Public Management*, and other publications. ICMA's efforts for the improvement of local government management—as represented by this book—are offered for all local governments and educational institutions.

About the Editors and Authors

Natalie Wasserman is executive director of the Public Risk and Insurance Management Association (PRIMA), a position she has held since 1979 shortly after the organization was started by the International City Management Association (ICMA). Ms. Wasserman holds an Associate in Risk Management (ARM) from the Insurance Institute of America and has a B.A. degree with a combined major in English literature and history.

Dean G. Phelus is a senior staff associate with the Public Risk and Insurance Management Association, where he has been responsible for the development and implementation of various programs and services. Previously, he worked for the U.S. Department of Housing and Urban Development. He received a bachelor's degree in political science and a master's degree in public administration from American University in Washington, D.C.

Following are the affiliations of the contributors to *Risk Management Today:*

David Brooks, Manager, Field Services, Ohio Local Government Insurance Plan, Columbus, Ohio.

Alex Brown, formerly Technical Services Coordinator, Colorado Municipal League, now Director of Research, Kirchner Moore & Company, Denver, Colorado.

Lauren C. Cragg, Staff Consultant, Tillinghast, Nelson & Warren, Darien, Connecticut.

David Dybdahl, Account Executive, Corroon and Black of Wisconsin, Inc., Milwaukee, Wisconsin.

Kurt Foerster, Marketing Manager, Alexander & Alexander, Richmond, Virginia.

H. Felix Kloman, Vice President & Principal, Tillinghast, Nelson & Warren, Darien, Connecticut.

David J. LaBrec, First Assistant City Attorney, Dallas, Texas.

James A. Landry, Associate, Mercer-Meidinger, Houston, Texas.

Don LeMond, Risk Manager, State of Missouri, Jefferson City, Missouri.

L. E. O'Brien, Executive Vice President, Associated Risk Managers of New York State, Albany, New York.

John C. Pine, Management Development Associate, Louisiana State University, Baton Rouge, Louisiana.

Ronald Rakich, Principal, Ronald Rakich & Associates, Austin, Texas.

Robert C. Vogt, Account Executive, Markel Service, Inc., Richmond, Virginia.

Robert W. Wennerholm, Police Legal Advisor, Fort Lauderdale Police Department, Fort Lauderdale, Florida.

Duane E. Wilcox, Senior Extension Associate, Local Government, Department of Agriculture & Economics, Cornell University, Ithaca, New York.

Charles Woods, Fiscal Advisor, Illinois Department of Commerce and Community Affairs, Springfield, Illinois.

Robert L. Young, Director of Risk Management Services, Arthur J. Gallagher & Co., Rolling Meadows, Illinois.

Contents

PART 4
Risk Control in the Workplace

PART 5
Conclusion

Introduction

Dean G. Phelus

Managing government is fast becoming a risky business. The erosion of sovereign immunity has made municipalities the target of a growing number of lawsuits, and the complexity of providing many services within budget constraints has made governments vulnerable to an ever-growing number of risks. Insurance has been one way of protecting a government against loss. In the early 1980s the insurance market was "soft," and coverage was both available and affordable. But in 1984, the market—abruptly and without warning—turned hard: premium increases of over 100 percent are not unusual, and some lines of coverage are unavailable at any price. In most cases, municipalities are receiving less while paying more; deductibles are higher and limits of liability lower.

A similar situation in 1978 prompted the creation of the Public Risk and Insurance Management Association (PRIMA) to act as an information clearinghouse on public risk management and insurance issues. Through its programs and services—which are intended to improve risk management professionalism in local government—PRIMA's membership has increased to over 950 public agencies, including states, cities, counties, school districts, highway authorities, and other special-purpose governments. This growth attests to the fact that risk management has come to play a major role in local government.

This book is designed to provide an overview of risk management by exploring its various components and special areas of concern. Material was selected to provide a basic understanding of the issues and to offer direction and ideas.

Part 1 focuses on the risk management function, providing an overview of the process and the steps involved in developing a risk management program. The opening article by Lauren Cragg and Felix Kloman outlines the major elements and objectives of a program and serves as the keystone for the rest of the book. L. E. O'Brien and Duane E. Wilcox then offer suggestions on implementation.

The next part explores options for financing risk. First, Ronald Rakich discusses bidding insurance for school districts and identifies various elements to include in bid specifications. David Brooks outlines the basic insurance principles that apply to property exposures and decisions that have to be made about how property insurance will be written. A selection from RIMCO Risk Management, Inc., looks at transferring financial responsibility through contracts and discusses some of the general areas that must be addressed by parties to a contract. Finally, Robert Young provides practical advice on the costs, advantages, and disadvantages of self-insurance, and Alex Brown explores self-insurance pooling by summarizing the steps taken in starting the Colorado Intergovernmental Risk Sharing Agency (CIRSA), the first municipal self-insurance pool in Colorado.

Part 3 looks at three areas of risk that have the potential to devastate a public entity financially: public officials liability, police liability, and environmental impairment liability. David LaBrec begins by summarizing civil rights exposures based on federal case law and suggests ways to minimize this liability. Kurt Foerster concludes that piece with a discussion of public officials liability insurance and its policy features. John Pine then offers tips on reducing the threat of personal and administrative liability. Robert Wennerholm suggests tactics and techniques that police can use to reduce the threat to their personal welfare and that of their community, and Robert Vogt offers a discussion of ways to prevent or control the liability involved in police enforcement. David Dybdahl concludes with an update on environmental liability and how best to handle pollution exposures given current market restrictions.

The focus then turns to controlling risk in the workplace through safety management practices, health care cost containment techniques, and workers compensation cost control methods. Don LeMond begins by discussing ways to integrate the safety function into the operation and management of government services. A case study of the safety program in Baltimore, Maryland, illustrates how safety can be achieved innovatively and inexpensively. Then the book turns to employee benefits, which are claiming an increasing portion of public budgets and are being incorporated into the risk management function. Tillinghast, Nelson & Warren offers some suggestions on how to contain health care costs. Then, in excerpts from a survey conducted by PRIMA and Mercer-Meidinger Inc., James Landry shows what employers nationwide are doing to manage health care costs. Public entities can have a direct impact in controlling costs in the claims area, too; Charles Woods provides a thorough explanation of ways to control workers compensation costs both before and after an incident or accident.

The concluding section offers comments from city managers and others who provide first-hand confirmation of the benefits and savings derived from their risk management programs.

In summary, this book guides the reader through the major steps of the risk management process. It emphasizes the importance of risk management to the financial security of public agencies and the health and welfare of the work force. Government exposures are numerous and costly, but, with the support and commitment of top management, they can be controlled, contained, and in some instances avoided by implementation of sound risk management techniques.

PART 1

Risk Administration

Risk Management: A Developed Discipline

Lauren C. Cragg and H. Felix Kloman

In July 1983, the Dallas *Morning News* featured an article forecasting risk management as the number one job for 1990.[1] On schedule with this forecast, the discipline of risk management in the governmental area has rapidly developed over the past few years.

Governmental entities and their public officials have been embroiled in severe financial and insurance difficulties because of the erosion of the official immunity doctrine and the rising tide of litigation in our society. Each day the press reports suits against public bodies, drastic increases in insurance premiums and deductibles, or outright insurance cancellations.

The insurance industry is partially to blame for this crisis. The inadequate underwriting practices of the late 1970s and early 1980s, reducing interest rates, and a failure to segregate municipal from other liability losses have contributed to the current crisis.

But much of the blame must be assigned to governmental bodies themselves. Insurance programs have been political footballs, bid far too frequently. Loss prevention programs have been inadequate or nonexistent. Resources have been wasted unnecessarily.

The result: a need for a new response. The erosion of governmental immunity to third-party liability suits, the lack of effective risk controls, the increasing cost of governmental insurance, and the fact that insurance companies are no longer willing to write governmental entities have all led to an increased interest in risk management, a process for developing practical solutions to these problems.

Revised and updated from "Risk Management: A Developing Discipline," by H. Felix Kloman, *Governmental Finance*, May 1977.

The risk management discipline has certainly received increased attention from governmental entities. Since its creation in 1978, the Public Risk and Insurance Management Association (PRIMA), a membership organization created to provide information on risk management and insurance, has increased its membership from an original 250 to over 900 members in 1985. Numerous municipal pools provide workers' compensation and/or property/liability insurance; the majority of these have been formed within the last five years. Municipal risk management has received the recent attention of the *New York Times*, *Forbes*, and *Business Week*. Today, the growing recognition of the importance of risk management can be seen in the acceptance of this discipline as a major governmental function and the placement of full-time risk management officers in many larger cities and counties. As a logical decision-making process devoted to conservation of resources, it can help governmental bodies to respond to some of today's problems.

The development of risk management is represented by the increasing visibility of risk managers as public officials, membership in governmental risk management associations (such as PRIMA), the number of municipal insurance pools, and networking channels among municipal associations (e.g., International City Management Association, National Institute of Municipal Law Officers, and Government Finance Officers Association).

Historically, risk management has been an outgrowth of insurance management. As buyers attempted to obtain insurance coverage on a more favorable basis, many recognized that insurance was but a step in a far broader management process.

The objective of risk management for any governmental entity is the conservation of its resources from accidental loss. These accidental loss exposures, affecting human, financial, physical and natural resources, are diverse and ever-changing, as are the risk controls and funding mechanisms available to meet them. Without a coordinated and continuous effort to uncover significant loss exposures, to apply reasonable and effective risk controls, and to ensure that the financial integrity of the governmental entity is not impaired after a loss, serious repercussions may result, particularly from taxpayers.

The elements of risk management include:

1. Exposure Identification: The creation of a continuous process of identifying the resources for which a governmental body is responsible and the accidental loss exposures that could materially affect them.
2. Risk Evaluation: The measurement of financial risk by analyzing past loss frequency and severity of individual and multiple government bodies, and by estimating future frequency and severity probabilities.

3. Risk Control: The reduction or elimination of risk or loss, within proper economic constraints, through careful procedures and practices in security, personal safety, fire prevention, auto safety, product safety, environmental protection, and emergency planning.
4. Risk Funding: The provision of sufficient funds to meet loss situations if they occur, by the most effective use of internal and external financial resources, including insurance.
5. Risk Management Administration: The development of administrative techniques to carry out the risk management process most effectively, using skills both inside and outside a governmental entity.

Exposure identification

The first step in the risk management process is the identification of governmental resources and the loss exposures that could affect them. Resources can be categorized as human, physical, natural, financial, and intangible. City halls, airports, bridges, cemeteries, hospitals, libraries, signs and signals, vehicles and contents are but a few of the physical properties owned by or entrusted to governmental bodies. Human resources include employees, officials, volunteers (police and fire) and skilled outside specialists. Financial resources include not only cash, checks, and securities, but also federal tax stamps for which a governmental body may be responsible. Where water is supplied, the availability of this natural resource from local streams, lakes, or deep wells can be extremely important to both taxpayers and customers. These diverse municipal resources and operations, whether governmental or proprietary, face exposures to loss from natural perils such as flood, windstorm or earthquake, and from more common perils such as fire, explosion, riot, collision, or vandalism.

Many direct exposures may also have indirect consequences for a governmental body, generally related to extra expenses that are incurred in order to maintain necessary operations or services. While mutual aid agreements are effective means of reducing these expenses, there are other costs that can cripple a governmental body. Many governments have income producing facilities whose earnings could be interrupted by a direct physical loss. Finally, a major area catastrophe, even if it did not directly affect governmental property, might have a significant negative effect on tax income.

Human resources are subject to death, disability, accidental injury, and sickness. The medical profession has cited smoking, drug addiction, alcoholism, and obesity as four of the most serious problems in the United States, all of which create serious problems for municipalities and their employees.

The most serious loss exposures in terms of both frequency and severity potentials, are third party liabilities. These losses can arise out of intentional or unintentional torts, statutory liabilities, and contractual liabilities. The continuing erosion of governmental immunity, the increasing exposure of public officials individually, the growing litigiousness of a highly affluent society, all coupled with inflation and changing social values, have created our current difficult situation.

Governmental bodies can be held responsible for accidents arising out of the use of owned or non-owned automobiles, watercraft, or other vehicles. In addition, the use by an employee of a personally owned or personally chartered aircraft may well create an exposure of enormous magnitude. Every contract, such as mutual aid agreements, leases, purchase orders, loans, construction contracts, and so on, may have hold harmless or similar clauses which transfer liability from one party to another.

New exposures are continuously arising in the liability area:

1. Suits may be brought for alleged environmental pollution, posing liability and risk management response problems. Jackson Township, New Jersey, was sued for negligence in its selection, design, and maintenance of a waste site that resulted in contamination of the local water supply.
2. In Baumstown, Pennsylvania, several city wells were contaminated by a municipal waste site. The contamination required a contingent water supply plan, which resulted in increased risk exposures. The city brought in tank trucks to provide water, but in cold weather the distribution sites resulted in an inordinate number of falls from ice caused by run-off from the water distribution. To eliminate the ice hazards of the distribution site, the city began to deliver the water to homes in steel drums, that also had a tendency to freeze in the cold weather. A large number of claims, ranging from rashes and illness to death, were also alleged to be results of the contingent water supply.
3. Another potential municipal exposure is the civil rights of prisoners. Allegations of improper conditions and inadequate medical treatment have resulted in a $2 million suit against the sheriff of Dutchess County, New York (on behalf of an inmate who died in Poughkeepsie Hospital), as well as a class action suit for inadequate health care, food, and conditions.
4. The city of Los Angeles was sued by 520 property owners near the Los Angeles International Airport, who claimed that the value of their property had been reduced by the noise created by airport operations. This type of claim is called "inverse condemnation."

5. Responsibility for workers' compensation insurance for persons volunteering community service is another potential municipal liability.

Since governmental resources and the exposures that can affect them are wide-ranging, any governmental body should institute a continuing program of identification through the use of checklists, questionnaires, interviews with department heads, and physical inspections of properties.

In addition to these internal sources, the governmental officer charged with risk management responsibilities may also obtain assistance from local insurance agents and brokers, insurance companies, the Public Risk and Insurance Management Association (PRIMA), the Risk and Insurance Management Society (RIMS, representing risk managers and insurance buyers throughout the United States), and other specialized organizations such as the Government Finance Officers Association and the International City Management Association.

Risk evaluation

Having identified exposures to loss and the resources which can be affected by them, the next logical step is to measure the financial risks inherent in each exposure in terms of frequency and severity. The objective is to devote the maximum attention to those exposures that may have the greatest potential financial impact on a governmental body. The first step is to assign a value to various municipal resources. Valuation is not easy, especially since few standards exist in government. The valuation process can be reasonably sophisticated in the case of real or personal property, where qualified appraisers can measure replacement cost or "actual cash value," the valuation basis most generally used by insurance companies. For items such as library books, however, a more subjective or average valuation may have to be used, taking into consideration not only the average replacement cost per volume, but also the cost to catalog and stack replacement volumes. Values, however determined, should be trended annually to keep pace with inflation.

The value of any resource includes the income, earnings, or cash flow generated by it that may be affected following a direct loss. It may include extra expenses if it is essential to continue an operation following a loss. For a data processing facility, for example, substantial extra expenses may be necessary to recreate damaged or destroyed media and to maintain the flow of data to users without interruption.

After a tentative value has been attached to particular resources, the municipal risk management officer should estimate the potential frequency and severity of every exposure. Some, for example earthquakes, may occur infrequently but have substantial potential severity. Others, such as vandalism to school buildings, may occur frequently, but with relatively inconsequential financial results.

The key tool in risk evaluation is the governmental body's loss history. This is a five-year history of paid and reserved insured and self-insured losses, showing both the number of losses and the dollar amount assumed by the municipality or paid by others. Complete records should be maintained for every type of loss (property, liability, crime, workers' compensation, etc.). For purposes of forecasting, the losses can be compared in each year to the most reasonable "exposure base," or more formal projections can be made. These exposure bases include payroll, operating budget, vehicle miles driven, and other indicators that have a relatively high correlation to past loss history. Whatever the recording method, it must be kept by the municipality, not only by insurance agents or companies.

Many municipalities are now using sophisticated quantitative skills in preparing simulation models and actuarial forecasts to use for better risk control, risk funding, and budgeting decisions. Others have created a computer-based risk management information system to maintain loss, exposure, and premium records. The relatively low cost and high capacity of personal computers have made them common tools in governmental risk management.

Judgment dictates that consideration be given not only to the worst possible loss, but also to the probable size of loss that might occur. Many organizations now use "maximum foreseeable loss" *and* "maximum probable loss" estimates for the total losses that can arise from a single occurrence. Maximum foreseeable loss is the greatest conceivable loss, assuming the failure of all preventive mechanisms. Maximum probable loss is the worst loss to be expected under "average" conditions, assuming that most, if not all, control mechanisms and procedures operate effectively.

Risk evaluation, like exposure identification, is a continuing process. While in some areas it may be subject to rather precise measurement (as in property values and cash exposures), subjective judgment will often prevail, as is the case when estimating public liability claims and losses. The five-year loss history remains the most useful tool for reviewing what has occurred in the past and helping to estimate what might occur in the future.

Risk control

After identifying exposures and evaluating financial risk, the governmental risk management officer can move to the most important step in the risk management process—risk control. The objective of risk control is the elimination and/or reduction of not only loss, but risk itself. A major problem within many governmental bodies is that the management of risk control is seriously fragmented and uncoordinated, controlled by different organizations such as the fire department, police department, and public works. As a result of this fragmentation, the risk control record of public bodies is seriously deficient.

For example, in 1975, according to the National Safety Council, the national average of lost time cases due to personnel injury was 13.1 per million hours worked. The chemical, aerospace, and automotive industries all had rates of less than 4, while federal civil employees had a rate of 6.5. The rate for municipalities, however, was 41.3! Police, refuse, and fire rates were even higher—54.8, 98.7, and 149! In other words, 1 of 14 municipal employees was involved in a lost time accident in 1975. One of 10 police employees, 1 of 6 refuse handlers, and 1 of 4 fire fighters were also involved. While there are perhaps extenuating circumstances to explain the police and fire records, the record for refuse and other municipal personnel was clearly the result of inaction and inadequate attention to safety.

In 1983, eight years later, according to the National Safety Council, the basis for incident rates had changed, from lost time accidents per million hours worked to a ratio of incidents involving days away from work per year. The rate for public employers, 5.95, was still more than twice as high as the all-industry rate. Police reported a 6.90 rate, fire 7.27, and refuse collection 18.81! While the difference between governmental and all-industry rates has been reduced slightly in eight years, the record remains very poor.

More and more municipalities are therefore recognizing that, to improve the record, a more coordinated approach is absolutely necessary. The risk control process involves:

1. Definition of risk control areas and development of municipal policy
2. Development of procedures for each control policy
3. Provision of constructive assistance so that each department can follow these procedures realistically
4. Monitoring of actual compliance on a periodic basis.

The elements of sound risk control for a governmental body will include:

1. Security: Protection of persons, property, and information from internal and external criminal activity
2. Personnel Safety: Meeting the requirements of federal and state occupational safety and health acts that set standards for work safety, the work environment, and record-keeping
3. Fleet Safety: Setting standards for vehicle safety and developing procedures to assure safe operations (for example, re-

view of driving records of employees who regularly drive municipal vehicles and enactment of stringent defensive driving courses)

4. Property Conservation: The protection of physical property from fire and other perils, with regular inspections by the fire department
5. Environmental Protection: The development of plans so that the disposal of solid, liquid, and gaseous wastes will comply with state and federal statutes
6. Emergency Preparedness: The development of contingency plans to anticipate and handle a wide variety of emergencies, such as bomb threats, natural disasters, fires, floods, and train derailments, and to ensure that such plans are brought up-to-date periodically. The Disaster Planning Guide of the Defense Civil Preparedness Agency is an excellent guideline. Coordination with the designated Civil Defense Officer can significantly improve emergency planning. Because of the potential severity of many types of emergencies, many believe that logical contingency planning is the *most important* area of risk control for any government entity.

Coordination of risk control activities under the aegis of the risk management officer is but the first step in mounting an effective risk control program. It is equally important to assign accountability for both risk and loss. Many municipalities now allocate losses to departments on an equitable basis so as to stimulate incentives for loss prevention. The actual performance records of individual public employees and departments must be measured against specific risk control goals.

Risk funding

The objective of the risk funding portion of a governmental risk management program is to make the best use of total financial resources so that sufficient funds will be available to meet loss situations as they occur. Despite even the most complete exposure identification and risk control program, new exposures still manage to appear; controls fail to achieve their intended purpose; and governmental bodies can still face the prospect of significant financial loss.

Objectives in risk funding include:

1. Providing sufficient funds to meet the worst possible loss event
2. Providing the maximum stability of risk funding costs over time
3. Taking maximum cash flow advantages in the operation of risk funding plans
4. Obtaining the lowest reasonable direct cost for risk funding

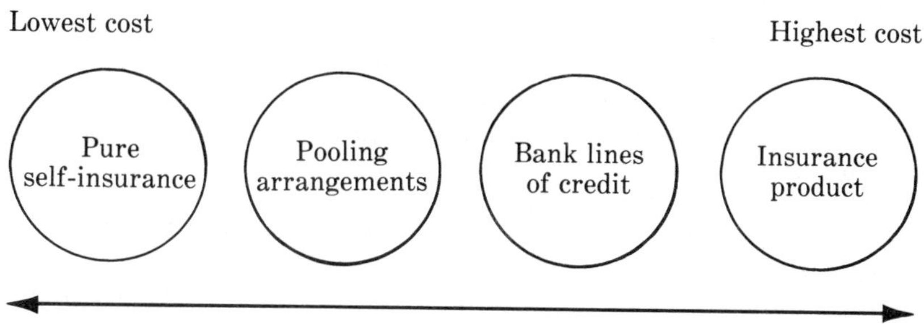

Exhibit 1. Least cost spectrum.

commensurate with the funds that are made available and the services that are offered by certain funding media.

What are these funding resources? A public body generally has access to a wider range of financial resources that private business organizations. These include (in relative order of cost—see Exhibit 1) direct expensing to various departments, using surpluses available within departmental budgets; funded or unfunded reserves, depending on the legality of such reserves; borrowing from financial institutions or increases in tax rates; federal funds (for example, from the Federal Disaster Act, Public Law 93-288); "pooling" or sharing risk with others in a self-insurance company or risk-sharing authority; and, finally, insurance. While insurance remains the most frequently used method of handling certain risks of accidental loss, it is by no means the only method or the least expensive. In the past, the greatest weakness of most municipalities has been an overreliance on insurance alone as a funding tool. Insurance is still one of the major resources for funding of governmental risk, but it is in short supply today.

Before considering insurance as a funding mechanism, a municipal risk management officer should define the capacity for risk retention of the governmental body. Perhaps no area is more important or more generally overlooked by most government entities. Simply because of financial size and spread of risk, any entity has an ability to retain the smaller or more recurring claims that can be predicted with some degree of assurance. Furthermore, if these smaller claims are funneled through the insurance mechanism, the costs can be extremely high.

Self-insurance is and should be a significant part of the risk funding program of any governmental body. A general guideline is that the governmental body should be willing to accept from one-tenth of 1 percent to one-half of 1 percent of its operating budget in uninsured losses arising out of a single occurrence, and up to 1 percent of its operating budget as the aggregate of all such self-insured losses in a single fiscal year. This guideline is considered prudent and should form the basis of a self-insurance "policy" for any organization. Today, many governmental bodies are self-insuring well in excess of this figure. For example, because of the high cost of insurance the state of Nevada decided to self-insure its public liability exposures entirely.

Not only are most municipalities assuming significant higher levels of risk through deductibles and outright self-insurance, but many are considering the feasibility of pooling on a local, regional, or state basis. In California, in the late 1970s, the cities in Contra Costa County pooled together for liability and property risks, largely on the basis of a significant change in the California law on October 1, 1976.

Section 990.8 of the Government Code was amended to permit two or more local public entities to purchase insurance under a joint powers agreement, or to pool self-insured claims or losses without becoming qualified as an insurance company or being subject to regulation under the Insurance Code. Earlier in 1974, the Texas Municipal League created a pool for Texas cities and towns.

By 1985, pools for workers compensation, property insurance and public liability have been set up in Alabama, Illinois, Texas, Florida, Connecticut, Maine, and at least 16 other states. Pooling has become the most significant development in governmental risk management in the past five years. PRIMA has developed a specific pooling section in response to this need and interest.

Some governmental risk managers are now recommending the creation of a multi-state mutual insurance company or reinsurance company to fund required levels of excess insurance for participatory pools. There is a real possibility that, by 1995, more than one-half of all governmental risk funding will be carried out through government sponsored pools and excess insurance companies.

Partial self-insurance can be practiced through the use of deductibles under property or liability insurance contracts, or through the use of other types of rating plans that permit sharing the risk with the insurance company. In any decision regarding risk retention, however, due consideration should be given not only to the premium credits available from insurance companies, but also to administrative savings services that may be provided by the insurance carriers and the long-term preservation of the insurance market.

The purchase of insurance itself requires a careful approach to the marketplace. The constriction of the insurance marketplace, particularly for liability insurance, has reached crisis proportions.

For example, in New York in June 1985, the largest insurer of municipalities in the state announced that it will not renew liability

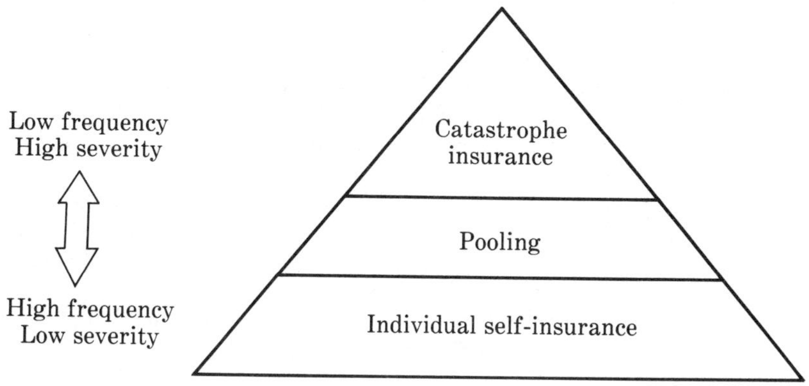

Exhibit 2. Protective pyramid.

policies for 229 local governments. Those that can obtain insurance must pay significantly higher prices—often for lower limits and higher retentions. One New York government entity saw its annual liability insurance premium jump 183 percent in 1985, to $822,000. Another saw its liability premium go from $109,871 to $349,833. These figures are part of a report issued by the New York Assembly Local Government Committee, which details what it calls a "financial threat that has entered a crisis state" for the costs of renewal premiums for municipalities.

Many states and municipalities have certain requirements for bidding insurance. Many insurance observers have indicated that frequent bidding has been one of the major causes for the restriction in the marketplace. Insurance companies prefer a longer-term relationship than one to three years. In general, it is preferable to *restrict* full bidding of required insurance to once every *six* years (or often two complete three-year policy renewal cycles).

Although the market has serious problems, most governmental bodies will continue to use some form of insurance, either on a primary or excess basis, to protect against catastrophic losses. Exhibit 2 shows the so-called "Protective Pyramid" in which individual self-insurance and pooling are combined with catastrophe insurance to provide proper protection for governmental bodies.

Generally the forms of insurance available to municipalities will include the following:

1. Property Insurance: This includes both fire and "all-risk" contracts on buildings, contents, and property in transit. "All-risk" protection may include collapse, water damage, earthquake, and flood in addition to the more common fire,

extended coverage, vandalism, and malicious mischief coverages. The familiar exclusion of riot and civil commotion, which became prevalent in the late 1960s and early 1970s, can now more generally be eliminated. Other coverages include boiler and machinery, business interruption, extra expense, and coverage on electronic data processing equipment and media.

2. Crime Coverages: These include both employee dishonesty and faithful performance bonds, some required by local statutes, and other protection against burglary, robbery, or theft. In particular, consideration should be given to crime coverage on the financial property of others (such as impounded cash or other valuables, and federal tax stamps) when these exposures exist.
3. Liability Coverages: These include all forms of public liability insurance, automobile insurance, workers compensation, and professional errors and omissions insurance. Umbrella or excess liability protection is essential, generally with a recommended minimum limit of $5 million. In general, liability insurance should be extended to include not only the governmental body, but all boards, commissions, elected officials, employees, and, in certain circumstances, even volunteers when acting on behalf of the entity. Following civil rights actions in the 1960s and early 1970s, many entities began to produce professional liability for police officers and public officials, but this market has eroded significantly in the past few years. Other professional liabilities include those of medical practitioners (doctors, surgeons, nurses, and emergency medical technicians), teachers, and engineers.
4. Employee Benefits: Generally these coverages will be coordinated with the personnel department, which defines the scope of benefits for health insurance, major medical insurance, long-term disability income insurance, accident insurance, group life insurance, and pension plans. Larger municipalities have undertaken self-insurance for certain types of benefits that have a relatively high frequency and low severity.

The risk management officer should apply some general standards to all insurance contracts:

1. Named Insured: The name insured should be consistent on all insurance policies and, in the case of liability policies as indicated above, be broad enough to include all boards, commissions, officials, employees, and others who may be acting on behalf of the governmental body.
2. Limits: Property limits should be related to either actual cash value or replacement value, taking care that coinsurance re-

quirements are met and that values are updated on an annual basis. There are certain statutory stipulations in various states for bonding requirements. For liability protection, $5 million is the absolute minimum for any municipality, of whatever size.

3. Notice of Cancellation: All insurance contracts should include provision for a *minimum* of 60 days' written notice by the insurance company before cancellation, nonrenewal, material increase in rate, or material reduction in coverage can become effective.
4. Participation in Risk: The risk management officer should give continuous consideration to participation in insurable risk by the use of deductibles, retrospective rating plans, and other self-insurance techniques, where available.
5. Loss Adjustment: All property losses should be settled with and made payable to the governmental body, and the requirement for proper notification of loss to the insurance company should begin only after the municipal risk manager or similar officer is made aware of a loss.
6. Expiration Dates: A municipality will generally find it advantageous to have as many of its contracts as possible expire on a common date, preferably coincidental with the fiscal year.
7. Premium Payment: Cash flow is an extremely important consideration in any risk financing program. While insurance policies may be issued for terms of from one to three years, it is possible to pay premiums on an annual, quarterly, or monthly basis so as to generate significant cash flow savings.

In summary, a risk financing program will reflect all of the financial resources available to a municipality, using insurance as only one of these resources.

Risk management administration

Whether a governmental body be large or small, the administration of a risk management program requires continuous direction and careful attention. For larger bodies, there will be a full-time management officer, perhaps with additional staff, particularly in the safety area. In smaller bodies, however, risk management will be but another responsibility for a finance officer. Nonetheless, even if the conscious consideration of a risk management program is restricted to but two or three hours of serious thought once a year, significant benefits can result from adopting this logical decision-making process. The following are considered to be the general requirements of an effective program:

1. Written Policy: The governing board should approve a writ-

ten statement or policy on risk and insurance management. A sample policy appears in the accompanying box.

2. Organization: Most states and many larger governmental bodies have now named full-time risk managers. Smaller municipalities have often combined the safety and insurance function. In many smaller governmental bodies, however, the prime responsibility for risk management will rest on the shoulders of the finance officer.
3. Responsibilities: Whether full-time or part-time, the governmental risk management officer will have responsibility for the normal steps of exposure identification, risk evaluation, risk control, and risk funding and will, as well, review major leases and contracts, coordinate other risk control efforts, process claims, and, under certain circumstances, work with the personnel department on the design and funding of employee benefits programs. The risk manager will also maintain the risk management information system and allocate costs, losses, and premiums.
4. Communications: Effective communication lines are essential and, for many municipalities, this will include a brief annual report to the governing board as well as a short "manual" for guidance of various departments and employees. Here too the computer-based risk management information system will be of assistance in communications with insiders and outsiders alike.

Sample risk and insurance management policy

[Name of city] is to be protected against accidental loss or losses which, in the aggregate during any financial period, would significantly affect personnel, property, the budget, or the ability of [city] to continue to fulfill its responsibility to taxpayers and the public. In no event shall any loss of life or major personal injury to employees or members of the public be acceptable.

[City] will apply to risks of accidental loss the risk management process which includes a systematic and continuous identification of loss exposures, the analysis of these exposures in terms of frequency and severity probabilities, the application of sound risk control procedures, and the financing of risk consistent with financial resources.

In recognition of its financial resources and the spread of its physical assets, [city] will accept retention of uninsured losses up to the following limits:

Not more than $[amount] arising out of a single event or occurrence; not more than $[amount] aggregate during any fiscal year.

Conclusion

The current liability insurance crisis is acting as yet another catalyst for a growing recognition on the part of many governmental bodies that risk management can be an effective means of conserving resources and avoiding unnecessary waste arising out of accidental loss. This recognition can perhaps be best summarized by the results of the risk management program of Santa Ana, California. Not only did the city realize significant financial savings in risk funding, but it found a "noticeable reduction in both the number of claims reported and in claim expense." The city's conclusion: "Continuous monitoring of risk causation factors and the implementation of safety and loss control programs, coupled with effective claims administration, are considered to be the ultimate solutions in reduction of injury claims and the costly economic impact on our cities." Risk management is indeed a developed discipline for America's states, cities, and towns.

1. *PRIMALETTER*, vol. 5, no. 10, September 1983.

Risk Management Organization and Administration

L. E. O'Brien and Duane E. Wilcox

The role of top decision-makers

Achieving a successful risk management program requires involvement by a local government's top decision-makers—the members of the governing board and top executive officials (such as the village or city mayor or manager, the town supervisor, the county manager or chairman of the legislative board) as well as other officials with influence beyond that indicated by their official titles (for example, a knowledgeable and respected county attorney or clerk of the legislative body). A number of things are needed from these decision-makers.

The basic requirement is their strong support for a risk management program. Achieving a successful risk management program will require that significant changes be made in customary ways of doing things. Officials and employees will have to do things that they haven't done before; they will have to *stop* doing other things that they are accustomed to doing; funds will be spent and accounted for in different ways; and relationships among local government officials and employees will be altered. Without a strong commitment from the top local decision-makers, expressed both in statements and resources for program implementation, it will be much more difficult and perhaps impossible to achieve such changes.

One way in which the support of top local decision-makers

From L. E. O'Brien and Duane E. Wilcox, *Risk Management: An Introduction for New York State Local Officials*, Local Government Program, Cornell University, Ithaca, N.Y., 1981. Prepared with financial assistance from the New York State Department of State and the U.S. Office of Personnel Management under the Intergovernmental Personnel Act of 1970. Copies may be ordered from the Local Government Program, 313 Warren Hall, Cornell University, Ithaca, N.Y. 14853.

should be expressed is in a formally adopted risk management policy statement. In addition to expressing top-level support, this statement should provide overall guidelines for the implementation of new practices. It should also serve to strengthen the authority of the person assigned primary responsibility for administering the program. Matters that might be covered in a policy statement include these:

1. An overview of the objectives of the risk management program (for example, protecting the jurisdiction from catastrophic losses, protecting the public and employees from serious injuries, minimizing the cost of accidental losses) and the methods to be used to obtain those objectives
2. The authority and responsibilities of the risk manager and the party or parties to whom the risk manager is responsible
3. The responsibilities of department heads and other officers and employees
4. Important procedures (for example, for reporting accidents and paying claims)
5. The jurisdiction's policy on insurance coverages (for example, exposures that will be insured and retained, levels of coverage and deductible amounts, and insuring of property for actual cash value or replacement cost)
6. Establishment and operation of a claims reserve fund
7. The establishment of a loss control program and the emphasis to be given to this effort
8. Records to be kept.

An alternative to adopting a single policy statement covering all of these matters is for the local governing board to adopt a brief policy statement of a general nature as a basis for the formulation by administrative staff of more detailed guidelines. In many situations, this may be a more efficient use of the time and energy of both legislators and administrators and may produce more consistent detailed guidelines than the give-and-take of legislative compromising.

In any case, the top local decision-makers should understand the principles and assumptions underlying the risk management guidelines. Without this understanding, the risk management program and those administering it may at times be subjected to unwarranted criticism. For example, a brief period of bad experience with claims could result in such criticism if members of the local governing board do not understand that risk retention must be viewed from a long-term perspective. Those who formulate and administer the guidelines should assume the responsibility for explaining them to key local decision-makers, both initially and at later dates, particularly when new persons assume key executive and legislative positions.

How to formulate a risk management policy statement

Some suggestions that you may wish to pursue, either singly or in combination, are the following:

Ask a committee of the governing board or an administrative official or perhaps a combination of the two to produce a draft statement for review by others.

Appoint a risk manager on either a temporary or permanent basis and ask this person to produce a draft statement. If he or she does not have a good background in risk management, allow a period of time for self-education.

Seek advice from the municipal insurance agent, the municipal attorney, and department heads and private parties with special knowledge (such as the risk manager for a local company).

Adopt a provisional policy statement to be modified later as everyone learns more.

Collect and analyze the policy statements of other jurisdictions and sample statements produced by writers in the field; consider how these statements should be modified to fit your situation.

Another major responsibility of top local decision-makers is to keep themselves informed on the progress of the risk management program and to help formulate overall program directions. One way to do this is by asking the risk manager for written reports at regular intervals (perhaps quarterly or every six months) and then discussing them with him or her and other parties with key risk management responsibilities, such as the municipal attorney.

Top local decision-makers must also develop a concern for the risk implications of their own decisions. Perhaps the best way for them to do this is to make a habit of asking themselves "What are the risk implications of this matter and the way we are considering dealing with it?" On many occasions, this should lead them to ask for information from the risk manager and other persons with special information. In addition, top local decision-makers should institute procedures for channeling information on matters they are considering to the risk manager and ensure that he or she feels an obligation to provide information on the risk implications before decisions are made. For example, minutes of meetings of the local governing board should be routinely forwarded to the risk manager if he or she does not attend these meetings on a regular basis.

Selecting and supporting a risk manager

How should a risk management program be administered?

Hiring a professional risk manager is an obvious alternative. Local governments with large populations should be able to justify the choice of this alternative because of their substantial resources and the magnitude of the task of implementing and continuing an effective risk management program in large jurisdictions.

A closely related alternative is that of expanding the duties of a safety director. Jurisdictions with this position have a natural base on which to build. Assuming that the incumbent is capable of becoming a competent risk manager, the responsibilities of the position could simply be redefined to include all aspects of risk management.

An alternative that merits serious consideration by smaller jurisdictions is the joint employment of a professional risk manager. County governments might provide a convenient geographic focus for such an arrangement, since the risk manager could serve not only the county but a number of the municipal governments within the county. Working out an agreement governing the hiring of the risk manager and his or her obligations to each of the employing jurisdictions would, of course, probably require a considerable investment of time by local officials.

The use of a risk management committee may seem to be another reasonable alternative for smaller jurisdictions, but this approach has serious shortcomings. An effective risk management program requires significant involvement by many different parties—the municipal attorney, the insurance agent, department heads, and so on. This fact may lead one to think that a risk management committee composed of these persons or their representatives is a second-best way of administering a risk management program.

It is certainly not impossible to achieve satisfactory results with this approach. But, in general, the committee approach is unlikely to result in the assigning to one person of a specific responsibility to learn a considerable amount about the discipline of risk management, to "push" others to implement risk management measures, to provide adequate supervision of a recordkeeping system. Without this leadership, other priorities will probably overwhelm the good intentions of most committee members and other officials and employees, and little will be accomplished. A better means of providing for accountability and clear direction is needed.

For smaller jurisdictions that cannot join with others to employ a professional risk manager, we recommend that a person already filling another position be designated risk manager and provided the incentives and support necessary to achieve a successful risk management program. Specifically:

1. The incentives might include a salary increase and an increase in the person's status within the governmental administrative hierarchy.
2. The municipality should authorize the risk manager to attend risk management training activities. It should provide a bud-

get for the acquisition of books, manuals, newsletters, and other resources that the risk manager will need for self-education, to keep current on new developments and information, and to assist with day-to-day risk management activities. The risk manager should also be allowed time to study these resources, especially at the outset of his or her new responsibilities.

3. If the person designated risk manager is someone other than a person with general executive responsibilities (for example, someone other than a city or village mayor or manager, a town supervisor, a county manager, etc.) or someone who already reports to such a person (for example, the budget officer), then provision should be made for the risk manager to report directly to a top executive person. This will emphasize the importance of the risk management program to all local officials and employees. It will also make clear to them that the risk manager can easily call upon a high level of authority for assistance if other parties fail to cooperate.
4. Transferring some of the previous responsibilities of the person designated risk manager to another position and providing clerical assistance can help this person combine the old and new job without assuming an unmanageable work load.
5. Top local decision-makers should communicate to local officials and employees that the risk manager is entitled to call upon them for assistance and that they have an obligation to respond positively. Individual officials and employees should be "on call" as needed by the risk manager. In addition, the risk manager may wish to call key persons together on a regular basis (perhaps two to four times per year) to review the overall program and to discuss particular matters needing attention. Those with a special obligation to assist the risk manager include the municipal attorney, the budget officer, and other persons with special expertise, such as in property appraisal (the assessor), safety (police officers and firefighters), engineering (the city engineer), etc.
6. Assistance should also be available from parties other than those in the direct employ of the local government. The risk manager should be able to count on the municipal insurance agent and the jurisdiction's insurance carriers for a substantial amount of insurance-related services (loss control assistance, annual reports to the governing board on losses and claims, premium forecasts, efficient claims procedures). In jurisdictions of quite small population, competent and substantial assistance from an insurance agent and insurance carriers will usually be essential, since part-time mayors and town supervisors will probably be the persons most often put

in charge of risk management. It may also be desirable to contract with other outside parties on a permanent or temporary basis. For example, a municipality might want to employ a consultant to help with the initial tasks of setting up a program and identifying and evaluating risks; claims administration services might be purchased on a permanent basis from a concern that specializes in this aspect of risk management. Finally, top decision-makers should attempt to arrange assistance for the risk manager from any risk management specialists employed by other local organizations—for example, safety and insurance specialists who work for a university or a large company.

The general responsibilities of a municipal risk manager are to identify, evaluate, and deal with the risk exposures facing or potentially facing the particular governmental entity. But what should the specific responsibilities assigned to a municipal risk manager be? The answer to this question should be carefully considered and decided by local decision-makers with their particular situation in mind. The following "typical functions of a risk manager" does, however, provide a useful list of possibilities for local decision-makers to consider:

1. Participating in the formulation of a risk management policy statement
2. Identifying existing facilities, conditions, and situations that may produce losses
3. Reviewing proposed facilities, programs, and other activities for risk management implications
4. Preparing recommendations and providing assistance in eliminating or minimizing losses
5. Providing for the establishment and maintenance of records relating to insurance coverages, loss and claims, and other important information
6. Analyzing loss information
7. Preparing recommendations concerning appropriate methods for funding potential risks, such as purchase of insurance, current expense funding, or use of a claims reserve fund
8. Negotiating insurance coverages
9. Adjusting claims and working with the insurance carrier, insurance agent, service company, attorney, and others in the defense and settlement of claims
10. Allocating insurance and other costs related to claims among departments
11. Ensuring that appropriate changes are made in levels of insurance coverage in response to changes in requirements
12. Establishing and maintaining a loss control program

13. Reviewing and analyzing state and federal legislation, regulations, and court decisions for implications for the risk management program
14. Communicating "upward and downward" and encouraging participation in the program by other local officials and employees.[1]

Before designating a risk manager, local decision-makers may want to consider what qualifications the risk manager should have. In jurisdictions of very small population, this may not merit much time simply because the list of potential candidates may be very brief. In jurisdictions where the list of possible candidates is longer and more attention to qualifications is therefore merited, careful attention should again be given to the local situation. Some qualifications that local decision-makers should consider are the following:

1. Interest in being a risk manager
2. Ability to learn how to fulfill new responsibilities without significant formal training
3. Ability to set up and maintain an efficient recordkeeping system
4. Ability to identify trends and draw practical conclusions from data, personal observations, and risk management literature
5. Ability to identify the risk management implications of legislation, regulations, and administrative guidelines
6. Substantial familiarity with the local government's operations, since the risk manager should construct procedures that will facilitate the identification of changes and potential changes in risk exposures and should know how to use local patterns of influence to achieve objectives
7. Aggressiveness, since the risk manager must be willing to deal with potentially troublesome situations before they result in problems and also because his or her duties may require intervention in situations that others may wish left alone
8. Tactfulness, to avoid offending other parties and thereby hinder the cooperation upon which much program success must be based
9. Ability to communicate effectively, because much of the risk manager's success in eliciting cooperation from others will depend on their understanding of what he or she thinks should be done
10. Ability to educate, because of the possible need to organize educational events for local officials and employees and to make presentations at such events.

If the available candidates fall far short of meeting the above or some other list of qualifications, local decision-makers may simply have to be satisfied with the most qualified person. A partial remedy for this less-than-desirable situation may be to provide for more support and assistance than a more qualified risk manager would need—for example, more involvement by a competent municipal attorney, the handling of claims by a claims administration company, or more use of outside consultants for setting up procedures.

A final note: is it an impossible task?

"Can we really hope to implement a successful risk management program?" That question may occur to many officials of smaller jurisdictions. The pervasiveness of risks, the myriad things that should be done as part of a risk management program, and the need to do them without the leadership of a professional risk manager can easily make the task seem overwhelming. "If only we had the resources of large local governments . . ." is likely to be a common thought.

If you suffer such doubts, you may gain encouragement from reviewing past accomplishments in your own and nearby jurisdictions. With little doubt, you will be able to identify locally proposed or state-mandated programs and projects that initially seemed to many local parties to be exceedingly difficult or even impossible undertakings, but which now offer testimony to the initiative and capabilities of local officials. Such local success stories have been achieved in innumerable instances by local officials without academic training or experience directly related to the particular task that they were assigned or chose to undertake.

In addition, it is worth remembering that implementing and administering a risk management program in a large jurisdiction is not an easy task either. Many large jurisdictions are finding their resources hard-pressed in this era of program cutbacks and public resistance to governmental spending. Also, as the population of a jurisdiction increases, so too does the magnitude of the task of organizing and administering a risk management program. Think, for example, of the number of risk exposures and the number of department heads, supervisors, and employees whose actions should be the concern of a risk manager in a city of 200,000 inhabitants or a county of 1 million.

Also, local officials of smaller jurisdictions should keep in mind that implementing a risk management program is not like building a fire station. There is not necessarily a huge sum to be paid out or a "last brick" to be laid before a local government can begin to reap the benefits. Rather, if local officials initially concentrate on identifying and doing "quick and easy" tasks, they may begin to receive a significant return on their investment within a few months or even weeks. For example, a local government might quickly discover that it needs to greatly increase the limits of its coverage for catastrophic losses, obtain public officials' liability insurance, enact and implement a prior notice law, and obtain certificates of insurance from contractors. These are tasks that a novice risk manager may be able to accomplish with relatively little effort; at the same time they should significantly increase protection against risks.

In summary, then, rather than focus on the seemingly endless list of things that should be done as part of a risk management program, local officials of smaller jurisdictions should:

1. Carefully lay the groundwork in terms of commitment from top decision-makers, basic guidelines, designation of the most promising person as risk manager, and provision of financial and other resources to support the risk manager's efforts
2. Identify an initial list of promising tasks to start with
3. Get started with these tasks
4. Make expansion and consolidation of the program a continuing high priority.

1. Taken, with minor modifications, from: Association of Washington Cities et al., *Public Agency Risk Management Manual*, 1978, p. 25. Handling employee benefit negotiations with insurance carriers is a major addition that some sources would make to the above list.

PART 2

Risk Finance

Taking the Mystery out of Insurance Bidding

Ronald Rakich

Many considerations come into play when a school district or educational service agency decides to bid for insurance. Some school districts are not required by law to bid insurance coverages or self insurance services. On the other hand, there are many valid and practical reasons for bidding. Among them, obviously, are to compare coverages, service reputations, and cost. The lowest bid is not necessarily the best, since it is virtually worthless if it leaves your district with large uninsured exposures due to insufficient coverage. Likewise, poor service can more than offset modest premium savings by causing additional expense and aggravation.

Although model bid specifications and guidelines are included in this article, in some cases you may choose to use the services of a professional to assist in preparing your bid specification. If so, that person should *not be a potential bidder.* Too many conflicts of interest arise. If you are getting advice from a board of volunteers or experts, that group should be made up of *insurance buyers* rather than insurance sellers. Be wary of allowing the formation of a local insurance monopoly. A number of public entities have been involved in anti-trust suits due to such practices.

There are as many different possible formats for bid specifications as there are organizations wishing to bid; no one way is the correct one. It is important, however, to follow certain principles. Be logical. Be thorough enough to give your potential bidders an idea of what you want, but, do not restrict their creativity with too many

Ronald Rakich, "Taking the Mystery out of Insurance Bidding," October 1983, pp. 8-14, *The School Administrator,* published by the American Association of School Administrators, Arlington, Virginia.

details. They may have a better idea that they would not be allowed to present if your specifications tie their hands.

Your bid specifications should include at least five components; general instructions, conditions, program desired, underwriting data, and proposal forms.

General instructions

General instructions should tell potential bidders what is expected of them. Although there is no set format, there are some things your bidder needs to know.

Bid notice Some entities may have local policies that require them to advertise notice of their intention to receive bids (see Figure 1). Notice information may also be included in specifications that are provided to interested bidders.

You may also wish to call several things to the attention of potential bidders. For example, you may wish to state your district's right to reject any or all bids. You may want to specify that the bid most advantageous to the district, not necessarily the lowest bid, will be the one selected and that bids that do not meet specifications will not be considered.

In your notice you may stipulate that the bidders have some leeway, provided the outlined conditions are met. In other words, you may wish to encourage creative or better ideas. Generally, when you take this approach, you should specify that alternative quotations will be considered only when clearly explained. You may also wish to say that they will be considered only if the specifications are met and the alternatives are submitted as an alternate bid.

Statement of purpose Your statement of purpose section should indicate why you are going to bid. It may be that you wish to consolidate your coverages under a common expiration date. If so, say it. If you are trying to cut down on the total number of policies you have and would like to consolidate these, you should indicate that fact.

If you have considered retention (deductibles or self-insured retentions), you can indicate in this section your general philosophy of assumption of risk. You can specify later in the bid document what retention or deductible levels you are willing to take for each specific line of coverage.

This section is also a good place to do a little public relations. You may wish to include a statement that you intend to stay with the selection program for at least three years. This will make the underwriters and other parties involved in preparation of the bid more comfortable in dealing with you.

Timelines It is important to establish timelines. Perhaps the eas-

The ______________________ (Independent School District, College, Regional Service Center, etc.) will receive sealed proposals not later than ________ p.m. ________ (day) ________ (month) ________ (year) at the administration building located at ______________________________ ______________________________ (street address and office number) ______________________ (city), (state). Address proposals to: ______________________________ (name and title of administrator, superintendent, etc.) The district is seeking proposals for the following:

Building and contents:	Property Boiler Flood and earthquake Scheduled property D.P. media Valuable records	(Select appropriate coverage)
Liability:	General liability Automobile liability Personal injury liability School professional liability Employee benefits liability Umbrella liability	
Automobile and mobile equipment physical damage:	Vehicles Mobile equipment	
Crime:	Dishonesty Faithful performance Money and securities Miscellaneous bonds	
	(Or any other line of coverage)	

Bids forms, specifications, and instructions to bidders may be obtained at the above address.

The ______________________________ (entity) reserves the right to reject any or all bids or any portion thereof and to accept the bid most advantageous to the district. Any exceptions to coverages requested in the specifications should be clearly explained in writing. Failure to meet all specified conditions may invalidate a proposal.

Bid proposals must be clearly marked on the envelope:

Bid proposal

______________________________ ______________________________

(Superintendent or Administrator) (Date)

Figure 1. Sample bid notice.

iest way to do this is to include a timetable in this section of the general instructions. You will want to let your potential bidders know when the specifications are being released, when they must be returned, when the proposals will be evaluated, when the bid will be awarded, and when the coverages will become effective.

Persons to contact Let your potential bidders know who they will be dealing with for further information and who will receive their bids. Give them a name and number to use to get their questions answered.

Proposal requirements If you require a specific proposal format, say so in this section. If you want more than one copy, let your bidders know. In this section you may indicate that delivery of the proposal is the responsibility of the bidder whether it be by mail or in person. Indicate that your district is not responsible for delays or failures of any other party. You may stipulate conditions for withdrawal of proposals. For example, you may wish to indicate that no bidder will be allowed to withdraw a proposal for a certain period.

In this section you may also stipulate conditions for the interpretation of specifications; consideration of the proposal; acceptance of the proposal.

Conditions

Qualifications of bidders and insurers Certain minimum qualifications may be stipulated. This could include such items as:

1. The size and experience of the agent's or bidder's professional staff.
2. Names and qualifications of parties providing services called for in the specifications.
3. A resume indicating experience of the insurer or representative with your type of organization.
4. Insurer's financial rating. You may wish to submit a requirement for a minimum Best's rating. However, don't exclude nonadmitted insurers, self-insurance administrators, and other potential bidders you may not be eligible for a Best's rating. Furthermore, you should not set your rating qualifications too high. They are not an absolute guide.
5. Errors and omissions coverage. All bidders should furnish evidence of errors and omissions coverage. This can be provided in a statement accompanying the proposal or in a certificate showing this coverage.

Services required In this section you should stipulate the general type of services required by these specifications. These could include, but would not be limited to:

1. Claims service. Indicate your requirements for response to a claim. Also, in this section you may wish to discuss your requirements for claims reports and loss runs. Do not make these too restrictive. Do not ask for information you don't need, only that which you need to manage your program.
2. Loss control services. You may request the bidder to submit a description of recommended services for safety and loss prevention. You may request information about facilities and staff your bidder has available to provide these services.
3. Administration. The special reporting requirements, settlement authority, and any other unusual requirements may be set forth in this section.
4. Valuation. If any services are required, such as property appraisal assistance or preparation of values this should be stated in this section.

Specimen policies In this section you may detail which policy specimens should accompany the bid. This should include unusual forms such as umbrella insurance. Although it may not be necessary to request basic coverage documents, unless you are bidding a standardized policy, it would be helpful to have them. Any manuscript (custom) policies should be requested. All endorsements should be required. These documents will be very important when comparing proposals.

Program desired

General requirements You can be as specific or as general as you desire in this section. Usually, general is better. If you are being served by a professional, you will want him or her to exercise some judgment and show some creativity. On the other hand, if you know exactly what you want, you should detail coverage and policy language. In most cases, though, a statement of goals serves the purpose just as well.

If you are bidding more than one line of coverage, you may wish to stipulate conditions applicable to all policies or plans. For example, you may wish to indicate that your entity will be the named insured. Pay attention also to naming individual insureds or groups of insureds such as the school board or employees where appropriate (for instance, errors and omissions policies). This is a good place to stipulate cancellation requirements. You may wish, for example, to require 60-day cancellation notice.

Some important considerations are the effective date of the coverage, paperwork requirements (such as binders, application forms, and so on), quotation terms (for example, whether or not all additional charges such as premium tax shall be included), and cost basis.

Property Property specifications should include limits of coverage designed for each area of potential loss, including direct loss for damaged property, indirect losses such as loss of revenues due to school closings, and extra expense losses such as the expense of renting classroom space when a building is destroyed. You should specify the method to be used for valuation such as actual cash value or replacement cost. The Texas Association of School Boards, for example, strongly recommends that districts consider replacement cost value except in situations where a building would not be replaced under any circumstances. It is not recommended that you stipulate an amount of coverage or coinsurance conditions. In terms of perils covered, we strongly recommend that all risk coverage be specified. In addition to basic property coverages, districts need to consider their need for boiler and machinery coverage. Many districts should have this type of coverage.

You may wish to specify a deductible or give the bidder the option of quoting different rates at different deductible levels. However, if you do this, it is important that you limit the number of deductible options you require your bidder to quote on. This indicates to the underwriters that you have given some thought to how much you are able to retain and that you are willing to share a portion of the loss. It also implies that you are concerned about loss control.

It is a good idea to stipulate what options or desirable conditions you would like to see.

Liability Many school districts have limited liability exposures defined by statute or by federal requirements and including coverage for accidents involving negligent operation of motor vehicles. Since districts enter into a wide variety of contracts, contractual liability should be covered on a blanket basis.

Professional liability of school boards and employees also needs to be addressed. This should cover acts, errors, and omissions of the district itself as an entity, the school board, all employees and administrators, and the superintendent.

Since personal injury liability is excluded in standard errors and omissions policies and in other types of liability policies applicable to school districts, it should be stated that this exposure must be covered.

Schools are immune from most other general liability exposures. Nevertheless, there is a very real exposure to defense costs. Your specifications should require that these contingencies be covered.

Umbrella excess liability is a good idea. It should be "following form." In other words, it should closely follow the coverage of the underlying policies.

If your district has any unusual exposures, these should be considered in detail as well. Examples are malpractice for medical professionals, fiduciary liability for trustees of a benefit program, product liability, and so on.

Automobile and mobile equipment Although automobile fleet liability coverage has been discussed under liability coverage, many districts choose to provide physical damage coverage to their vehicles and mobile equipment. Often, this is overdone. Many districts that can afford to retain small property losses do not, more as a matter of custom than as a carefully thought-out policy. If your district has a need for physical damage coverage to driver education cars, for example, stipulate the need in your specifications. Carefully consider your deductibles. One hundred dollars may not be the best choice. Many districts do not carry physical damage coverage at all, but choose to retain the risk and make their own repairs. Physical damage coverage, of course, applies to damage to your own vehicle not caused by a liable third party. In other words, it's your problem.

Crime coverage Most political subdivisions are required to obtain faithful performance bonds rather than honesty bonds. You should specify minimum limits required. In Texas, two individual bonds are required for a tax assessor-collector and a textbook custodian. All other employees can be covered by a blanket faithful performance bond.

Money and securities are another area in which districts may or may not choose to purchase coverage. If your risk management analysis indicates that you can tolerate a loss as large as your maximum possible dollar loss, don't purchase money and security coverage. If you are not sure, leave some room for optional quotes in your bid specifications.

Employee dishonesty coverage should also be considered. This covers loss of money, securities, or other property—losses your district may face through fraudulent or dishonest acts of employees. This can also be covered under blanket bonds.

Underwriting data

In this section you want to tell the underwriter as much as possible about your district. Your intent should be to give a clear picture of whom they are dealing with. Of course, you will want to put your best foot forward. Some of the items that should be considered in this section are:

1. Any report describing your entity. This could include a general descriptive paragraph, an annual report, or anything else

Property	**Insurer**	**Annual premium**	**Average annual rates**
All risk			
Named peril			
Replacement cost option			
(Special options)	( )	( )	( )
Automobile and mobile equipment physical damage			
Boiler and machinery			
Liability			
General			
School professional (E & O)			
Automobile			
Personal injury			
Employee benefits			
Contractual			
Crime			
Employee dishonesty			
Faithful performance			
Money and securities			
Tax assessor-collector bond			
Textbook custodian bond			
Separate policies			
Not included in above (e.g., floaters)			
Total (Indicate included options)			

Please indicate any exceptions to specifications on an attached sheet. Check here if sheet is attached.

Signature of bidder ________________ Title ________________

Company ________________ Address ________________

Tele. no. ________________ Date ________________

Figure 2. Sample proposal form—property/liability package.

you may have. It is a good idea to include financial statements as well.

2. Lists of everything your district owns, with values. This could include buildings, vehicles, a list of boilers, and mobile equipment. In many cases, this will be available from your current carrier.
3. All employees by title or classification. You do not need to list individual names, but the underwriter should get a good idea of what different types of people work for you. This is especially important in workers' compensation and errors and omissions coverage, but has importance in fidelity and crime coverage as well. It is a good idea to list your trustees also.
4. A detail of accounts receivable exposure.
5. Any items available from your current carrier such as current policies, experience rating information, and so on.
6. Miscellaneous items such as valuable papers, fine art, or band instruments.

Any loss information that you have should be attached to this section. Normally, this will be available from your current carrier by line of coverage. However, some districts keep their own records on this subject. If you have that information, provide it.

Although it seems like a lot of work to gather this information and make it available, it is worth it. The more information the underwriter has, the more favorably they will look on your district. Attention to detail pays off when your rate quotations come back.

Proposal forms

Designing a proposal form makes it easier to compare quotations and also makes it easier for the bidder to make sure they have "covered the bases." There are many different formats that can be used. Design your own or use Figure 2.

Conclusion

Preparing bid specifications really isn't all that mysterious. It just takes a little attention to detail and a willingness to ferret out information. Keep in mind one important concept in going to bid. That is the idea that you are "marketing in reverse." You are trying to sell the underwriter on your district.

The suggestions presented here are not all encompassing, nor are they universally applicable. Use them as you would any other suggestions, and modify them as you wish.

Property Insurance

David Brooks

Insurance on your buildings and contents is probably the oldest form of insurance that you have carried. Although it has been around the longest, property insurance isn't as cut and dried as it might appear to be. You can make more decisions about how to handle your property insurance than most other forms of insurance. These decisions are important because they will determine how much coverage is provided and the cost of the coverage.

Your entity has various types of property. Property can consist of buildings and contents, unlicensed equipment used by the street and utility departments, boilers, electrical machinery, computers, and cash and negotiable securities. However, regardless of the type of property, there are fundamental insurance principles that apply to most of your property exposures. This article will first discuss these basic principles and relate them to your buildings and contents. However, it should be kept in mind that these concepts also apply to your other property exposures.

The first basic concept is being aware of the property. This isn't as easy as it sounds. When we go into entities to do our risk management surveys, we often find property that the entity was not aware of, or that was inadvertently uninsured. One common problem is one of your departments going out and renting additional space, or making some major equipment purchase, without telling the appropriate person. The solution is to first have one person for the entity being responsible for administering the insurance program. The next step is to establish procedures so that all departments are re-

Reprinted with permission from the January 1982 issue of *Ohio Cities and Villages*, published by the Ohio Municipal League.

quired to inform the appropriate people about any purchases. Also, the entity can use information generated by the required audits of property to make sure that the property exposure is known.

Another main concept concerns having accurate values for the property. This is crucial to your entire insurance program. Before making any decisions, you have to know how much is exposed to loss, and whether the property is concentrated at one location or is spread evenly through numerous locations. Having accurate values amounts to knowing what you are insuring before deciding how to insure it. One method of establishing accurate values is to have appraisals made on the property. There are numerous companies willing to perform property appraisals and there are also some insurance companies and private individuals that are willing to perform appraisals. Some appraisal companies will also provide periodic adjustment of values to make sure that the values are keeping pace with inflation and other changes. Regardless of who establishes these values, it is important that they be updated at least annually.

The next four areas concern decisions that will have to be made about how the insurance is to be written. We will be referring to these as the four decision areas. You should be aware of these, because they can determine whether or not there will be coverage and how much of the loss will be paid by the insurance company.

Decision area one—scheduled or blanket basis

The first decision concerns choosing between a policy written on a scheduled basis or a blanket basis. We are referring to the way the property is listed. Most policies are written on a scheduled basis, and if the policy doesn't say blanket, it is scheduled. For scheduled property, you are listing the property and you have separate limits of insurance for each location and its property. It is possible to have one location underinsured and another location overinsured. Part of the solution is to have property written on a blanket basis. Here we are still listing the property and listing values, but the amount of insurance refers to the total property limit. You eliminate the problem of one location being undervalued. However, having accurate values are still important, because you still want an accurate total limit.

Decision area two—named peril versus all risk

The second decision concerns named peril versus all risk. By peril, we mean cause of loss (fire, windstorm, etc.). On a named peril policy, you are listing the perils that are insured. Normally, we would be talking about fire, windstorm, and vandalism and malicious mischief. The other approach is an all risk policy. This is a very broad policy insuring against all losses except those specifically excluded. With an all risk policy, there are less disputes in settling a claim.

With a named peril policy it is up to you to prove the loss is covered. On an all risk policy, it is up to the insurance company to prove that it is excluded.

Decision area three—actual cash value or replacement cost

The third decision involves whether to insure the property for its actual cash value or replacement cost. Actual cash value is replacement cost less depreciation. If you insure the property for its actual cash value, you will have to assume the depreciation on any loss, regardless of how much coverage you have. This is important for older buildings as depreciation can be quite high. Replacement cost is the cost to replace the damaged property with new and like quality. The policy will pay for what it costs to replace the property, up to the policy limits. No deduction is made for depreciation. Making this decision illustrates the importance of having accurate values. An appraisal will give you the replacement cost and the actual cash value. You will know the amount of the depreciation and then you can make an intelligent decision about whether to retain the depreciation and insure the building on an actual cash value basis, or insure for the full replacement cost.

Decision area four—coinsurance or an agreed amount clause

The last decision concerns choosing between coinsurance and an agreed amount clause. Incidentally, the first three decisions relate to most of your property exposures, but the decision between coinsurance and agreed amount relates mainly to your buildings and contents. Most policies have a coinsurance clause. This clause requires you to insure the property at least to 80 percent of the actual cash value or replacement cost value of the property. If you don't you will suffer a penalty above and beyond depreciation at the time of a loss. The insurance company estimates what you should have carried at the time of the loss. If you have a coinsurance clause and you underestimated the building value, there will be a penalty.

The alternative is to purchase an agreed amount clause. Here you eliminate the possibility of a coinsurance penalty. You and the company agree in advance what you should carry. Then the loss will be paid in full, less any applicable depreciation and deductible. Many entities have a problem with the coinsurance limit that they have selected. They simply are not insuring for the values required by their coinsurance clause. However, merely purchasing the agreed amount clause is not a solution to underinsurance. In return for the use of the agreed amount clause, many companies will require some evidence that the buildings are insured at their proper limits.

The use of deductibles

Another subject that applies to all types of property concerns the use of deductibles. We often see a $100 deductible for the buildings and contents. I believe that you should at least consider a $1,000 deductible or higher, and see the difference in cost. To put the subject of deductibles in perspective, think about our homeowner's deductible. A $100 deductible is common. I question using the same deductible for our homeowners policy as we are using for values of $5 million, $10 million, and higher. In considering a deductible, you should look at the frequency and severity of past losses, how much the city or village can afford to retain, and then look at the premium savings.

Indirect losses

There are two major types of losses, direct losses and indirect losses. We have been talking about losses to buildings and contents. These represent direct losses, for the loss suffered by the entity is due to the peril physically contacting the property. The other type of loss is an indirect loss. An indirect loss results from a direct loss. Extra expense is the most common type of indirect loss that an entity faces. Some services such as police, water, sewage treatment, and road repair are essential and must be provided. In case of a loss, the city will incur extra expense to keep the operation going. The extra expense could be for rental of buildings, leasing of equipment, buying services from other entities, cost of moving, overtime, etc. Extra expense insurance would cover these extra expenses that exceed the normal operating expenditures. In deciding whether or not to purchase the extra expense, consideration should be given to whether or not the operation is essential, how difficult it would be to keep the operation going, and if back-up services are available. Going back to our four decision areas, the decision between schedule or blanket would be particularly relevant to extra expense. You could have extra expense on a blanket basis, covering all property, or you could list a particular location where it is to apply.

Now we will return to direct exposures. The next type of property exposed to loss is inland marine or floating equipment. This refers to property that doesn't remain at a fixed location. Examples would be tractor mowers, backhoes, graders, and other unlicensed equipment used by the street or utility departments. Also included in this category would be portable tools (compressors and pumps) and portable radios. All equipment in this category should be insured on an equipment floater. We often find unlicensed road equipment on an automobile policy. We would recommend putting the equipment on the equipment floater. The property protection for the equipment can be insured at a lower cost with broader protection, on the equipment floater. The liability for the equipment will be covered automatically under the comprehensive general liability policy. Again, we need to go back to the four sets of decisions. We have to choose between scheduled versus blanket, named perils versus all risk, and actual cash value versus replacement cost. Agreed amount clauses are generally not used for equipment floaters.

Another type of property exposure is valuable papers. Here we are talking about maps, deeds, manuscripts and drawings. The main exposure is the cost of research to recreate the papers. The all risk policy on the building and contents would exclude the cost of research needed to duplicate the papers. Valuable papers coverage is needed for this exposure. This exposure can also be treated by loss prevention, in lieu of or in conjunction with insurance. You could have a duplicate set of papers at another location, or possibly have them on microfilm stored at another location.

Boiler and machinery

The boiler and machinery is another exposure. The main boiler exposure is explosion. Even with a small boiler, an explosion can do a tremendous amount of damage to the building and also to surrounding property. It is important to know if your boiler is a hot water or steam boiler. Damage caused by an explosion of a hot water boiler is covered under the all risk property policy for the building. Explosion of a steam boiler is not covered under the building policy, and a boiler policy is needed. Also, if you desire coverage for damage to the boiler that is confined to the boiler, such as sudden cracking of the tubes, a boiler policy is needed regardless of the boiler type.

Occasionally we hear someone tell us that boilers are not required to be inspected, since they belong to a government entity. We should realize that all boilers are required to be inspected annually by either the state or an authorized insurance company. Current certificates of inspections must be posted in boiler rooms.

A second part of the boiler and machinery exposure is machinery. Included in this category would be fired and unfired vessels, air conditioning systems, motors, pumps, and miscellaneous electrical apparatus (control panels). Machinery values could be quite high at certain locations, such as the sewage treatment plant and the water plant. The machinery would be covered under the building and contents all risk policy. However, certain objects are exposed to additional perils, such as electrical surges or sudden burn outs that are excluded under the all risk policy. A machinery policy would cover these additional exposures. In deciding whether or not to cover the machinery, one should consider the frequency and severity of past losses, the value of the equipment, how much the entity depends on the equipment and the ability of the entity to retain possible losses. For example, entities often find that it is more economical to retain the loss exposure to pumps under 25 horsepower due to their relatively low cost.

Coverage for electronic data processing equipment

Another category of property that is exposed to loss is electronic data processing (EDP). We are talking mainly about computers. Again, this property would have the same coverage as that for other buildings and contents under the main property policies. However, some EDP equipment is especially susceptible to losses that are excluded under the main property policy (excess humidity, sudden electrical surges, and temperature change). The EDP would cover these additional exposures, along with all other exposures except for those few that are specifically excluded. If there is an EDP policy there is no need to have the equipment covered under the main property policy. For leased equipment, it is important to look at the contract to determine who is responsible for maintaining the insurance. It might be possible for the vendor to assume responsibility for coverage under the lease.

Another EDP related exposure is the software or the program. There could be a large extra expense in reestablishing the program. In evaluating the exposure, you would have to look at what the software is used for, how essential it is, and how much it would cost to replace the media. Part of the EDP policy could be used to cover the extra expense in recreating the data. This would be referred to as "media coverage." Again, loss prevention can be used in lieu of, or in conjunction with the media coverage. It might be possible to store a backup program at another location or have the vendor to store a backup program.

Another EDP exposure involves the extra expense in getting the computer back into operation after a loss. Included in the extra expense could be renting computer time, renting equipment, overtime, and other temporary expenses. Part of the EDP policy could provide for the extra expense needed to get the computer back into operation. In evaluating the need for the extra expense coverage, again you would have to look at what the computer is used for, how essential it is to keep it operating, and the availability of backup equipment in case of a loss. Again, going back to the decision areas, decisions regarding ACV versus replacement cost and specific schedule versus blanket would apply to the EDP exposure.

The last major property exposure is crime. The crime exposures fall into two basic categories. The first category is employee dishonesty. Some entities have large losses in this area. Some departments, such as the treasurer, clerk of courts, and the utilities, handle a significant amount of cash. There are other exposures in addition to embezzlement of money. Employees have access to expensive tools and equipment. A public employee dishonesty policy is necessary to cover this exposure. Employees that are required by statute to have public official bonds are excluded from coverage under the public employee dishonesty policy. It is important to keep the public officials bonds in effect, if they are required by statute.

The second category of crime exposure would be the destruction and disappearance of securities. The main property policy excludes coverage for loss of money and securities. Money and security exposures consist of safe burglary, holdup, and robbery of employees going to the bank to make deposits. A money and securities policy would protect loss of money and securities inside and outside the premises. Of the four decision areas covered before, the main decision applicable to money and securities would be to provide coverage either on a blanket basis or listing the specific locations to be covered.

Before summarizing, there is another important point about your property insurance program. We need to talk about how the property insurance relates to your total insurance program. By combining the property coverage with your general liability, your city or village can take advantage of a generous package discount. This could mean substantial savings in your premium. Considering the tight budget that we are facing and the cost of your total insurance program, the savings become even more significant.

We have reviewed basic concepts of property insurance, and how they relate to the various types of property that your city or village may have. It should be evident that you have many options available to you in handling your property insurance. Making the right decisions can mean significant savings in insurance costs and having the needed protection.

Risk Management in Contract Analysis

Virtually every business is required to sign contracts of various forms. In addition, many businesses require contracts to be signed by others. Contracts create important obligations and impose various conditions, rights, and responsibilities on the contracting parties. From a risk management standpoint, contracts must be recognized as a major means for transferring or assuming risk. It is, therefore, very important that when a business signs a contract which is presented to it by another party, such transfers of risks and other responsibilities and liabilities are carefully identified and acknowledged. With regard to the firm's own contracts which it offers for others to sign, it is important that any attempts to transfer such liabilities have been adequately effected through the structure of the contract and that the other party will be financially capable of responding.

The following is a discussion of some of the general areas which parties to a contract should address in the analysis of contracts. It is intended to give the reader general guidelines for contract analysis.

Analyzing contracts

The analysis of contracts can be a difficult and tedious process. Every clause or condition in a contract should be examined as to its ultimate effect upon the agreement being executed. As a general rule, contracts should be reviewed for any exposure to a contingent financial obligation. A "contingent financial obligation" is a finan-

---

Reprinted from the April 1981 issue of *The Risk Report* with permission of the publisher, International Risk Management Institute, Inc., Dallas, Texas. This report was written by RIMCO Risk Management, Inc.

cial obligation that will have to be met by the contracting party, given the occurrence of specified circumstances. For example, if the contract makes one of the parties liable for bodily injury damages to a third party, a contingent financial obligation is created. If the third party is injured (the contingent event), then the indemnitor must satisfy the financial obligation. In this context, it can be seen that any condition of the contract, the breach of which would constitute default, should be subjected to scrutiny, particularly if damages and procedures in the event of default are stipulated in the contract.

Thorough analysis of a contract is difficult to achieve. This is especially true when the individual analyzing the contract is not a lawyer. It is, therefore, desirable that the analyzer should:

1. Have a general awareness of risks and liabilities created by contracts in order to establish priorities and develop a proper perspective.
2. Have specific knowledge concerning the legality of the contractual provisions used to transfer risks or otherwise create contingent financial obligations. Understanding the ways insurance contracts respond to such liabilities and obligations is also critical.
3. Develop standards by which the liabilities and obligations contained in the contract can be evaluated as to their acceptability.

From a risk management standpoint, in most cases, the highest priority should be given to the identification of indemnity and/or hold harmless agreements, responsibility for damage to property of others, and requirements for insurance or other provisions in the contract which could have a direct effect on either the applicability or the enforceability of an insurance policy covering the exposure. At the next level of importance are conditions of the contract, the breach of which constitutes default; the rights of the parties and damages owed in the event of a default; and provisions which affect the duties and liabilities of the parties in the event that the contract is otherwise cancelled. Finally, unusual conditions and requirements should be examined and instances identified in which the contracting party must be responsible for procuring the services of another party. The major problem areas and their risk management and insurance treatment are presented here.

Indemnity

Indemnity or hold harmless agreements are used to transfer the ultimate financial responsibility for a given contingency to another individual. There are three general classes of Indemnity agreements which are defined as follows:

1. Limited form. The indemnitor agrees to repay the indemnitee

for any loss which the indemnitee sustains as a result of the sole negligence of the indemnitor.

2. Intermediate form. The indemnitor agrees to repay the indemnitee for any damages sustained as a result of the joint negligence of the two parties or the sole negligence of the indemnitor.
3. Broad form. The indemnitor agrees to repay the indemnitee for any damages sustained whatsoever, regardless of the negligence of either of the parties.

Some form of indemnity agreement will probably be found in most contracts. There will normally be a clause which applies broadly to the entire agreement. There may also be indemnity provisions in other clauses of the contract referring to specific obligations or contingencies. These indemnity provisions can create large potential liabilities. The problem is further compounded by the fact that in some cases, this contractual transfer of liability is not covered under a standard general liability policy.

Indemnity and hold harmless agreements

A general indemnity and hold harmless agreement usually reads as follows:

> The contractor hereby agrees to protect, defend, indemnify and hold the city and its employees, agents, officers and servants free and harmless from any and all losses, claims, liens, demands and causes of action of every kind and character including, but not limited to, the amounts of judgments, penalties, interests, court costs, legal fees, and all other expenses incurred by the city arising in favor of any party, including claims, liens, debts, personal injuries, including employees of the city, death or damages to property (including property of the city) and without limitation by enumeration, all other claims or demands of every character occurring or in any ways incident to, in connection with or arising directly or indirectly out of this contract. Contractor agrees to investigate, handle, respond to, provide defense for and defend any such claims, demand, or suit at the sole expense of the contractor. Contractor also agrees to bear all other costs and expenses related thereto, even if the claim or claims alleged are groundless, false or fraudulent. This provision is not intended to create any cause of action in favor of any third party against contractor or the city or to enlarge in any way the contractor's liability but is intended solely to provide for indemnification of the city from liability for damages or injuries to third persons or property arising from contractor's performance hereunder.

Source: David LaBrec, *Basic Contract Recommendations for Texas Cities* (Austin: Texas Municipal League, 1984).

Contractual liability coverage for lease contracts is included in the standard general liability policy. However, damage to property leased to the insured or in his care, custody, or control is excluded. The contractual liability created by hold harmless provisions in other types of contracts would, for the most part, not be covered unless the general liability policy is endorsed to cover contractual obligations of the type included in the contract.

On the other side of the coin, those who are attempting to transfer risk through hold harmless provisions need to be certain that:

1. The wording of the provision does not violate any state or local statutes which have been written to protect the public against indiscriminate use of such provisions.
2. The party assuming the risk or liability under the contract is capable of responding through insurance or other financial means if the loss occurs.
3. In the event the other party is not able to respond financially to the loss, the transferor will be able to cover the loss through insurance or some other means.

Indemnity or hold harmless agreements shift the ultimate financial burden of a loss, but they do not shift the responsibility for the loss itself. In some cases it may be possible to actually shift the initial responsibility for the loss in the contract. Clauses waiving certain duties or obligations can have this effect. For example, the contract may state that the lessor waives any responsibility for injury or damage to the lessee or his property.

Any wording in the contract which uses the term "waiver" should be carefully reviewed for:

1. The legality of the waiver
2. Any transfer of risk which may be effected by the waiver
3. Any waiver of subrogation.

One important legal issue to be considered here is that it is often not permissible for parties to a contract to define their legal rights, particularly with respect to liabilities and obligations to third parties.

A special case in the general area of waivers occurs if a waiver of subrogation rights is required under the contract. It is not uncommon to find the contract requiring a party to waive its insurer's rights of subrogation against the other party. The problem with this is that most insurance policies contain a basic policy condition stating that subrogation rights will not be waived by the insured unless written permission is granted by the insurer prior to the loss. The granting of such a waiver without the written permission of the insurer is grounds for refusing payment under the policy. Therefore, it is very important that both parties make sure that if a waiver of subrogation is required, the conditions of the respective insurance policies are not violated.

Provisions for damage to property

Many contracts, particularly lease contracts, will have provisions stating the responsibilities of the parties with regard to damage to their property. When one party has a stronger bargaining position, or is the sole drafter of the contract, there is a tendency to make the other party completely responsible for damage to the drafting party's property, while, at the same time, waiving the drafting party's responsibility for any damage to the property of the other party. Contracts will often contain a clause which specifically refers to this subject. However, provisions having a direct bearing on these responsibilities will be found in other parts of the contract as well, including the indemnity sections, the insurance section, and the provisions which dictate the condition of the property upon the completion of the agreement.

Wording can often be found in contracts which specifically states that the weaker party is responsible for loss of or damage to the stronger party's property, regardless of negligence or cause. In addition, such contracts may also contain a provision stating that at the termination of the agreement the property is to be returned in the same condition as it was at the commencement of the lease. Often the wording, "wear and tear excepted," is also added. However, the problem is that should the premises be destroyed by fire or other major casualty beyond the control of the lessee, the lessee will not be able to return the premises in the same condition as received, less wear and tear. It is, therefore, very desirable to have wording such as the following added to the Return of Premises clause:

> . . . excepting loss or damage from fire or other major casualty or act of God or cause otherwise beyond the control and/or not caused by the sole negligence of the lessee.

Insurance requirements

Many contracts have a section which dictates certain coverages and limits as well as endorsements and other modifications with regard to insurance required of the signing party. Certificates proving the existence of this insurance may be required. Often, the contract will require that written notice of cancellation or change be given to the other party by the insurer. Additional requirements such as naming the other party as an additional insured or obtaining waivers of subrogation may also be included in the insurance requirements section. The insurance requirements section, therefore, should be reviewed to be certain that:

1. Coverages and limits required are met by the present insurance program.

2. The individual arranges for certificates of insurance and other such endorsements as are required in the insurance requirements section.
3. The total insurance program of the signing party is adequate to cover the risks created by the contract.

It is also important to ascertain that the requirements set forth in this section are reasonable and possible to achieve. It is not uncommon to find requirements in this section which do not make sense and which cannot be met in a literal sense. For example, one contract recently reviewed required the individual to purchase general liability insurance covering "fire and extended perils." This is obviously, a misuse of terminology which could conceivably create some problems in the event of a loss.

Default, cancellation, and miscellaneous exposures

After the major problems of indemnification, waivers, damage pro-

Types of insurance

Some of the types of insurance with coverages with which cities are concerned (and which should be required of contractors) include:

1. *Workers' compensation coverage.* Insurance to protect against claims by employees who are injured while performing work for the city or contractor. Workers' compensation coverage should also be obtained for volunteers.
2. *General liability insurance.* Insurance to protect the city and its officials and employees from claims which arise out of bodily injury liability, property damage liability, advertising injury, or other occurrences or offenses. The coverage should require the insurer to defend the city and its officials and employees even if the allegations of the claim are groundless, false or fraudulent. The insurance should also cover premises and operations as well as contractual liability exposures. The amounts of general liability coverage should be determined by analyzing the city's legal exposures and prior claims history. It is recommended that the city purchase this kind of insurance only from persons who have specific prior experience insuring other Texas cities and city officials.
3. *Automobile liability insurance.* This coverage, like general liability coverage, should cover bodily injury and property damage. It should include owned automobiles, hired automobiles, and non-owned vehicles. Limits well above the Tort Claims Act limitations are recommended.
4. *Errors and omissions liability coverage.* This is coverage which protects public officials and employees from claims and suits which are made against them because of their actions (or inac-

visions, and insurance requirements have been addressed, it is desirable to review the contract for any other provisions which create a contingent financial obligation. In general, it should be recognized that breach of a contract provides the basis for a loss which may result in substantial damages being owed to the injured party. It would stand to reason, therefore, that any and all of the provisions of the contract must be reviewed in evaluating the possibility of a breach. Where conditions exist which cannot reasonably be fulfilled, some consideration should be given in terms of realistic performance requirements as to what the effect will be if either party attempts to bring an action for breach of the contract.

When the contract involves the payment of rent or some sort of fee, it is important to determine whether or not the party paying the fee will be liable for the total value of the contract if for some reason the contract is not completely fulfilled. For example, with respect to a lease of premises, it is not necessarily true that if the premises

---

tion) in the furtherance of their public duties. Members of boards and commissions should also be insured under the coverage.

5. *Personal injury liability coverage.* This is sometimes referred to as "police-professional" coverage, but it is much broader. It should include coverage for false arrest, detention, false imprisonment (police claims), as well as libel and slander, wrongful entry or eviction, invasion of the right of privacy, and similar claims. This kind of insurance should protect not only police officers, but also the mayor, city council, all other officers, employees, and volunteers who may be subjected to these types of claims, as well as the city itself. Limits of liability should be determined in the same manner as for general liability insurance.
6. *Contractors and consultants professional liability.* This coverage protects against liability which may arise from professional activities of contractors or consultants such as architects, engineers, accountants, attorneys, physicians, and so on. Proof (a certificate of insurance) of such insurance should be a condition of the contract for the professional services.

All proposed insurance agreements should be reviewed by both the city attorney and the risk manager and approved by each before they are presented to the city council for approval. The contracts should be read and understood—do not rely upon representations and statements made by insurance agents. Once the contract is signed, any representations that were made by agents are not binding: the written contract controls.

Source: David LaBrec, *Basic Contract Recommendations for Texas Cities* (Austin: Texas Municipal League, 1984).

were to be destroyed by an earthquake or some other casualty, the lessee would be released from liability for the payment of the rent during the remainder of the contract period.

Other examples of exposures to contingent financial loss could include a requirement to pay double or triple damages for a hold-over of premises beyond the term of the lease. Contractors and other service companies may be faced with provisions in contracts which impose heavy penalties for delay of performance.

Contracts may sometimes have unusual requirements such as the responsibility of one of the parties to provide security services, or render services beyond the normal standard of care. Such provisions may create a whole new set of liability exposures for the individual responsible.

Guidelines on bid specifications and contract negotiations

Below is a list of questions which should be considered in formulating bid specifications or in negotiating a contract.

What are the services to be contracted? By whom are they to be provided? (The services should be clearly defined in writing.)

What is the consideration to be paid? (The Texas Constitution prohibits cities from paying amounts which exceed the fair price of services or product being provided under the contract.)

What is the method and time of payment? (Are there going to be periodic payments? A lump sum payment? When will these payments be made?)

What are the inception and termination dates? In other words, when does the contract begin and when are the services to be completed? (It is suggested that automatic renewal provisions whereby the contract is automatically renewed without any action on the part of the city should not be used.)

Where are notices to be sent? (It is preferable that the contract contain provisions setting forth the location where notices are to be mailed and the person who is responsible for receiving and giving required notices on behalf of each party.)

The contract should require that the contractor comply with all applicable ordinances, regulations, and state and federal laws.

What insurance is needed to protect the city?

Will there be an indemnity and hold harmless agreement?

Are any bonds for payment, performance, bidding, etc., needed? Who are the approved sureties?

Will subcontractors be allowed to perform all or part of the work? What remedies will the subcontractors have against the city?

How can the contract be modified? (Many contracts contain pro-

Evaluating the exposure

The allocation and distribution of risk is an important part of the contracting process. The parties to the contract should take great care in addressing the risks created by the contract and come to an explicit agreement as to who shall bear the risks. One of the great problems encountered is evaluating the cost of risk arising out of a contract in determining the acceptability of a given venture. This is particularly true when the risks created are of a low frequency, high severity nature. While there is no easy method for quantifying the cost of risk as input to an economic business decision, the following principles and guidelines can be useful in the contract negotiation and/or evaluation process.

It should be recognized that with regard to contractual transfers of risk, there are two major areas to be considered. The first area deals with responsibility or liability for damage due to injury

visions that "This contract can only be modified in writing," although the provision has no binding legal effect. It is suggested that the city require that contract modifications may only be made with prior approval of the city council.)

What remedy will be available to the city in the case the other party breaches the contract?

Will contract disputes be resolved by arbitration, mediation, or in court? (It is recommended that the city not limit its remedies to arbitration or mediation. Those remedies will always be available unless the contract limits them.)

If a suit arises out of the contract, where will it be litigated? (It is suggested that a provision requiring that any lawsuit arising out of a contract dispute be filed in the state district court in the county where the city is located.)

Under what law will the contract be interpreted? (It is suggested that a provision be included whereby the contract will be interpreted according to your state's law.)

Where will the contract be performed? (It is recommended that the contract specifically provide that it is performable in your city and state.)

The contract should be dated and signed by an authorized representative of both parties. It is preferable that the contract be executed by the mayor or chief executive officer and attested by the city secretary or city clerk.

The foregoing is a sampling of some of the considerations which should be considered and thought out carefully in negotiating in preparing bids for a contract. It is by no means all inclusive, and city officials are encouraged to expand or modify it as needed.

Source: David LaBrec, *Basic Contract Recommendations for Texas Cities* (Austin: Texas Municipal League, 1984).

to third parties. The second area consists of responsibility or liability for damage due to injury between the contracting parties themselves.

Simply stated, common law would generally, in the absence of a contract between parties, make each individual responsible for damage caused by his negligence. This, then, should be seen as the starting point in contract negotiation. Any contractual provision which imposes a greater responsibility on the individual than would be imposed by common law should be addressed with additional consideration. Recognition that the assumption of additional responsibility through contracts bears a significant cost is an important first step in evaluating the acceptability of such contractual provisions. The important point is that the risks and liabilities created in the contract should be recognized and the magnitude of the risk should be considered as a relevant cost in deciding whether or not the proposed agreement represents a viable business decision.

Summary

In contract negotiation, it is very important that the two general areas mentioned above be recognized and specifically addressed by the contracting parties. In general, the most equitable treatment for all parties concerned would be for each party to be responsible for damages to third parties caused by his own negligence. Also each should agree to be responsible for and insure against damage to their own property, except perhaps for that damage caused by the sole negligence of the other party. It may not be possible to induce a stronger party in terms of bargaining position to accept this arrangement. However, in some cases it may be that the parties intend and agree that one of them should assume the additional responsibility. Addressing the problems in this way will establish a "give and take" process during the contract negotiation and should have a beneficial effect regardless of the decisions made concerning these issues.

Self-Insurance

Robert L. Young

Self-insurance has existed as long as man. Whenever someone would take a chance, knowing what the results could be, that person was, in effect, self-insuring against the chance of loss. In the world of commercial insurance, self-insurance has been most commonly practiced for workers compensation exposures. In fact, history shows that on the pirate ships that sailed the high seas, the captain would often give an additional share of the plunder to those of the crew who were injured while attacking another vessel. Today, self-insurance is practiced in many ways. Many companies adopt self-insurance or a similar form of cash flow program to reduce the cost of insurance. This article will examine self-insurance to determine:

1. What self-insurance is
2. Who should consider self-insurance
3. Why self-insurance should be used
4. When self-insurance should be used
5. Where to self-insure
6. How to implement a self-insurance program.

The costs, advantages and disadvantages, potential problems, possible solutions, and other features of self-insurance will also be discussed. Sources for more information will also be suggested for those who wish to explore the subject further.

What is self-insurance?

Self-insurance is probably one of the most widely practiced tech-

Reprinted from the December 1984 issue of *The Risk Report* with permission of the publisher, International Risk Management Institute, Inc., Dallas, Texas.

niques in the discipline of risk management. Given that an objective of risk management is to protect a company's assets and earnings in the most effective manner for the least possible cost, then self-insurance is one of the primary tools.

Self-insurance may be defined as a planned program of paying from a company's own funds for losses sustained, where it recognizes reasonably the potential losses that might be incurred, does all that it can to avoid or reduce this potential, and then provides a means to process and pay for the losses remaining. This does not mean that the purchase of all insurance is avoided. The organization will most likely require some protection against catastrophic losses or an unexpected frequency of losses. It would buy excess insurance against these possibilities.

Most importantly, self-insurance is a planned program. That is: all alternatives have been examined; self-insurance has been selected as the most effective device for the organization; all the necessary services to conduct the program have been arranged; loss funds are provided; excess insurance has been considered; there has been an attempt to recognize what problems might occur; and methods to monitor the progress of the program have been established.

Who should consider self-insurance?

First, self-insurance is not for everyone. It should be undertaken only by those firms that are large enough to assume a risk, that can reasonably predict future losses, and that would enjoy some economic advantages from a successful program.

Self-insurance is most successfully utilized for workers compensation, automobile liability, general liability, some specialized forms of liability (e.g., professional or malpractice), and for some employee benefit programs such as hospitalization, medical, and accident and sickness. To a lesser degree, it has been used for property, group life, and long- and short-term disability. It is most applicable to those coverages whose claims have a time value connected to their payment.

Workers compensation and automobile liability generally require permission from state agencies before self-insurance may be undertaken. Formal applications must be submitted to each state and be approved prior to the start of a self-insurance program. Therefore, the geographic spread of operations to be included in the program must be considered.

Today, most excess coverages apply above a $100,000 retention for each loss (in many states, this figure is substantially higher) or at an amount equal to the normal insurance premium of a fully insured program for aggregate protection against the combined total of all losses. Thus, if anticipated annual losses are less than the premiums charged for excess insurance, a self-insurance program would be more expensive.

Generally, for those coverages requiring state permission, the entry level is an annual premium of at least $250,000. This amount will vary, based on the industry, number of employees, location of operations, and the rates charged for insurance coverage.

Sometimes, an employer may consider self-insuring more than one type of exposure, such as workers compensation, automobile liability, and general liability, in one program where the combined premium base would be large enough to make such a program feasible. Organizations whose operations are spread over a large geographic area may find the paperwork required by numerous state agencies to be prohibitive and will seek one of the other alternatives such as paid loss retrospective plans, captive insurance subsidiaries, or similar approaches. Smaller employers often consider forming a group or association self-insurance program. These are permitted in a number of states, although some, including California and Texas, have not yet passed enabling legislation to permit them.

Again, before beginning a self-insurance program, conduct a study to determine if you can:

1. Obtain better control over your loss potential
2. Improve the processing and cost of claims
3. Save money.

Why should self-insurance be used?

Actually, the preceding paragraph leads into the reasons why self-insurance is sometimes a good method of handling loss exposures. When an employer first self-insures, he quickly becomes aware that the dollars being paid out every day are his (they were his when he paid an insurance premium, but the insurance company made the payments, and he usually did not have the same awareness of them as being his). He wants to do something about this outflow and perhaps will recognize that some of the money he will save through self-insurance can be spent to better protect against loss through more effective safety programs or hiring a safety director or using safety consultants to improve the company's loss record. He may even obtain improved employee morale through greater safety consciousness on the part of management.

Since the program is now his and not the insurance company's, he can arrange for the most effective claims processing system that fits his organization. If he needs claims professionals who are sensitive to employees and their personal problems or who have a language specialty or are more skilled at dealing with the public, he can hire them. He can find the service source that will be most responsive to the problems and needs of his particular company. For instance, he may be able to reduce litigation by requiring more direct and specific communication with claimants. He may choose to accept a borderline claim from the company's top sales representative whereas an insurer might have denied it and caused severe operational problems. He may decide to resist a claim that he feels is fraudulent whereas an insurer might have made a small settlement to eliminate the matter, thereby setting a precedent of which other employees might take advantage (perhaps dramatically increasing the losses sustained).

Self-insurance gives the employer an opportunity to have more firsthand contact with employees, letting them know that their injury claims are being paid for by their employer and not some distant, "rich" insurance company. The self-insured employer can: (1) expedite payment of benefits; (2) obtain a more accurate appraisal of claims costs; (3) decide the merits of each individual claim; and (4) exercise the amount or degree of control that he wishes using internal or external sources or a combination of both.

An effective and well-run self-insurance program should generate significant savings to the organization in comparison to conventional insurance plans. The costs and possible savings will be discussed later.

When should self-insurance be used?

Self-insurance should be considered whenever it would provide better control, better claims results, and significant savings over all other alternatives for the protection mentioned previously. A proper analysis of the costs, risks, and value of each method of protecting an organization's assets must be done before initiating any program. One of the most commonly used devices is a feasibility study. While such a study primarily focuses on the cost differentials among the choices available, consideration must be given to other factors such as geographic spread, state regulations, loss exposure, employee relations, public image, status of current safety efforts, and available resources to implement and operate the selected program.

When interest rates are high, the investment potential from reduced expenditures should be considered. A company's tax situation should be examined. In difficult economic times, if you can qualify, there may be a gain from reduced employee complaints as there will be greater concern about their jobs. In good times, when firms are expanding, self-insurance may free up funds to assist in the expansion, but an organization faces the possibility of unknown potential loss from new operations.

Whenever self-insurance can save money and result in improved control, it should be considered.

Where to self-insure

Self-insurance should be considered in any jurisdiction where there would be a savings, where the jurisdiction permits self-insurance and the organization can qualify, or where it can participate in a group program that is the most economical alternative. While there does not seem to be a state that prohibits self-insurance of general liability or employee benefits programs, several either restrict or do not permit self-insurance of workers compensation or automobile liability. For example, North Dakota and Wyoming prohibit self-insurance of workers compensation, while Texas will permit it only for public agencies (i.e., cities, counties, school districts, etc.). Most states have restrictions on the minimum size of automobile fleets that are acceptable for liability self-insurance.

How to implement a self-insurance program

The following steps are recommended to analyze and implement a self-insurance program. This is not a complete list but only an outline. A much more thorough analysis may be necessary for your organization:

1. Conduct a feasibility study to evaluate the costs in comparison to other alternatives.
2. Should the study show that self-insurance is the most economical approach, determine who should provide the necessary service functions.
3. Select the service provider or providers for claims, loss control, management information, financial, and other portions of your program.
4. Plan how to communicate to all members of the firm that the organization will be self-insured and establish the internal procedures to be used in the program.
5. Make any necessary applications to state authorities for approval of the program (this process may take some time, so allow enough lead time to file, provide additional information that may be requested, and obtain permission).
6. Arrange for medical services to include emergency treatment, specialists (e.g., ophthalmologists), and hospital facilities. You might also want to begin a program of preplacement physical exams (as well as continuing health standards) to properly place employees in positions for which they are most physically qualified.
7. Choose appropriate legal counsel for defense of claims. This may be one firm that becomes thoroughly acquainted with all of the organization's operations or many different attorneys chosen for their expertise in specific kinds of cases.
8. Make arrangements to receive the kinds of information needed to properly measure the progress of the program whenever it may be needed, in the form needed, and that it is accurate.

9. Determine the kind and amount of excess insurance and surety bond needed for the program.

There are many sources to assist you if you wish to pursue self-insurance. You can obtain help from risk management consultants, brokers, agents, insurers, independent service companies, state agencies, and many self-insurance associations. Most states have a state self-insurance association, and there is the National Council of Self-Insurers in Chicago and the Self-Insurance Association of America in California.

In brief, the advantages of self-insurance include direct control of losses, ability to provide the same protection at lower cost, and an opportunity to improve employee and public relations. Disadvantages include the inability to deduct the full cost of the program for tax purposes, loss of insurer services (which may be replaced by other sources), and the risk of the program costing more than an insured plan. If a self-insurance program is not properly protected through excess insurance, poor loss experience could result in costs that dramatically exceed the premium that would have been paid. In today's insurance marketplace, there are many insured plans that compete favorably with self-insurance. Eleven states now permit insurers to offer competitive workers compensation rates (open rating), rather than the standard rating programs that are fixed by industrial class code and prior industry experience.

In calculating the cost advantages, if any, of self-insurance, a feasibility study is usually conducted. The intent of a feasibility study is to compare the cost elements of the various alternatives applicable to a specific situation and, assuming the nonfinancial aspects are equal (the need to analyze these cannot be overemphasized), choosing the most cost-efficient alternative.

Self-Insurance Pooling Arrives in Colorado

Alex Brown

On January 1, 1982, the Colorado Intergovernmental Risk Sharing Agency (CIRSA) became a reality and commenced operations. CIRSA is the first municipal self-insurance pool in Colorado.

While self-insurance has been practiced by some individual communities in the state, CIRSA represents the first collective effort and offers a self-insurance plan to communities lacking the size to sponsor their own plan. This article traces the program's development and explains its benefits over the conventional insurance market.

Common insurance problems

The development of CIRSA was not prompted so much by the experience of any one community, but rather by collective problems with liability insurance experienced by a number of communities. The impetus for the plan had its origins in the mid-1970s, when a national recession had an adverse impact on the insurance industry. When insurance companies experienced significant underwriting losses, many communities either had their policies cancelled or were advised that renewal would require an increase in their premium, often in excess of 100 percent.

Many communities felt the price increases were unjustified in light of their claims history. A search for replacement coverage, however, revealed that many companies previously offering insurance in critical liability areas—e.g., police, professional, and errors

Reprinted with permission from the March-April 1982 issue of *Colorado Municipalities* magazine, published by the Colorado Municipal League, 1500 Grant Street, Suite 200, Denver, Colorado 80203.

and omission—no longer offered such coverage to municipalities. Consequently, the needed insurance was no longer commonly available at a reasonable cost.

Other common problems experienced by many municipalities involved claims adjusting. Several communities identified two basic concerns: inability to secure documentation of their loss history and an unwillingness of insurance companies to disclose policy concerning settlement of claims.

Many municipalities stated that insurance companies did not supply them with information concerning claims that had been filed or paid against their policies. Without such a documented claims history, communities could not identify the loss history of various operations and departments. Since many communities attempt to allocate insurance costs by department, the absence of a loss history frustrated this budgeting practice. Also, without data to identify departments or activities contributing to claims, cities could not improve safety programs and loss prevention activities in order to reduce their insurance losses.

The settlement of claims by insurance companies raised additional concerns for Colorado municipalities. In many instances, claims against communities were settled on the basis of the lowest cost rather than on the merit or principle involved. Many communities felt that frivolous claims were settled with a short-term outlook on immediate costs that ignored the long-range costs associated with the principle of paying that type of claim.

Many municipalities were also concerned about their inability to purchase complete insurance coverage. Often, when communities purchased insurance policies, they assumed that all public officials were covered for all aspects of liability. Unfortunately, this was not true. The deficiencies in coverage were often not detected until claims were filed and the insurance company refused to pay the claim. One area typically refused coverage involved alleged violations of civil rights. Federal and state court decisions and statute changes continually broadened municipal liability, but insurance policies did not always reflect these increased exposures.

Realizing these gaps in coverage, many municipalities purchased additional policies in an attempt to get more complete coverage. When the state league asked municipalities to produce copies of policies, they usually produced one- or two-inch thick notebooks containing as many as a dozen policies, each with separate terms, conditions, definitions, and limits of dollar coverage. This multitude of policies only added to the confusion; the insurance companies often sought to shift liability to one another, while the municipality was forced to review several insurance contracts in an effort to determine coverage.

Many conventional insurance policies involved a complicated

administrative requirement. In many cases, policies insuring property and vehicles required significant detail concerning the insured items, including valuations and serial numbers. For larger municipalities, this constituted a significant amount of paper work and any omission of proper value, numbers, and types of vehicles created a technical gap in insurance coverage.

Problems such as these were common for municipalities not only in Colorado but across the nation. Because the situation was more critical in California than in most other states, self-insurance pools were created there during the late 1970s. California's experience demonstrated that there was an alternative approach to purchasing insurance on the conventional market and proved that self-insurance pools can provide cost savings.

The Colorado Municipal League Executive Board, recognizing the problems being experienced by Colorado municipalities, felt there was merit in investigating alternative approaches to conventional insurance. The board authorized basic research in this area at its November 1979 meeting. This initial research was funded by the league and a grant from the Intergovernmental Personnel Act.

Phase I: Investigation

The initial research examined two basic questions. First, are the basic economics such that an insurance pool would be a feasible alternative? Second, what would the basic costs and structure of an insurance pool be for Colorado municipalities? The second question involved the identification of specific budget items and the amounts to be spent on each item.

Recognizing that this research would require the technical knowledge of both conventional insurance markets and self-insurance pooling, the league sought a qualified consulting firm. The league wanted a firm with no ties to the insurance marketplace. This meant that the firm selected could not sell insurance policies in addition to providing consulting services. A committee of municipal officials considered several firms and then selected the consulting firm that best served its needs.

The initial task was to compile insurance data from as many municipalities as possible. A survey was mailed to approximately 50 communities; 21 communities were able to compile the necessary data. This information included a three-year history of premiums paid, the dollar value of claims paid, deductibles carried in various insurance areas, an explanation of losses in excess of $25,000, and other data concerning the municipalities' operations and budget.

This data was assembled and analyzed by the consultant to determine whether the experience of Colorado municipalities and the aggregate dollars being spent were such that an insurance pool could be created. This was necessary since the league did not begin with an assumption that creating a pool was possible but, instead, with the desire to investigate this possibility.

The initial study revealed several facts concerning current liability insurance coverage and experience at that time. The insured loss ratio (the value of claims paid expressed as a percent of insurance premiums) was 44 percent over a three-year period. The total value of claims paid (to include deductibles) resulted in an experience ratio of 55.1 percent over the same three-year period.

Deductibles paid by municipalities on similar policies varied greatly. Some municipalities had purchased first dollar coverage while others had deductible clauses as high as $25,000. Conversely, in other liability areas, municipalities had no choice since insurance companies offered only policies with minimum deductibles as high as $5,000.

Some communities indicated that insurance was not in force in certain areas, such as liability for police professionals, thereby exposing them to the full cost of any claim filed in that area. It was also shown that most of the communities did not purchase liability insurance coverage above $500,000. A few communities had purchased umbrella liability insurance policies up to $2 million.

Review of findings

The consultant's research and analysis report was published in August 1980 and was disseminated to all participating municipalities as well as several other communities that requested a copy. The data demonstrated that pooling was economically feasible, and the consultant recommended that the league proceed with the formation of a liability insurance pool. In September, interested communities met to review the findings. At this time, the consultant explained the analysis and reasons behind various recommendations. Communities were asked to examine the data on their own and to determine if they wished to continue to pursue the establishment of a self-insurance pool.

At a second meeting held in November, interested communities decided to pursue formation of a pool. Each community was asked to express its intent to participate in the second phase before January 14, 1981.

Since the initial study had benefited and was available to all league members, general resources of the league had been used to fund part of the project. However, since the second phase would benefit those communities actually participating in the implementation effort, its cost was funded by a 10¢ per capita assessment to each participating community.

By the January 14 deadline, 26 municipalities had decided to participate in Phase II. This was five more communities than participated in the original study group.

Phase II: Decision making

The self-insurance study group, comprised of one representative from each of the 26 participating communities, met January 23, 1981. Goals were set for the coming year, including the ultimate goal of implementing a pool on January 1, 1982, and the original consulting firm was retained to assist in the second phase effort.

A steering committee was created to provide general guidance to both the consultant and league staff during this second phase. The full group reserved the right to make major policy decisions with recommendations from either the steering committee or a committee created for a specific purpose. Committees created by the steering group included a by-laws committee, a service selection committee, and a bank selection committee.

The by-laws committee collected and reviewed the by-laws of other self-insurance pools in order to identify matters that might be included in CIRSA. It was decided that the by-laws would also serve as the basic intergovernmental contract that would be adopted by each member municipality. By-laws were drafted that set forth the rights, duties, and obligations of each pool member. These by-laws also included the purpose of the organization, the powers reserved to the membership as a whole, powers to be exercised by the board of directors, a procedure for election of the board of directors, and procedures for the addition of new members.

The service selection committee was confronted with a different and perhaps more challenging task—to recommend qualified firms to provide services in three basic areas: insurance brokerage, loss prevention, and claims administration. The consultant prepared a questionnaire that was sent to approximately two dozen qualified firms. Responses were analyzed by the service selection committee and the consultant, and the committee selected three firms for each of the three areas. These firms then spoke to the entire study group, explaining their company's experience and qualifications.

Based on these interviews, the study group selected three firms to provide different services: insurance brokerage, loss prevention and data processing services, and claims investigation and adjusting.

The study group's next task was to finalize specific aspects of the program and to coordinate the activities of each firm. The broker conducted a preliminary investigation of the reinsurance market to determine terms and conditions. Based upon this market search as well as the data compiled by the consultant during the first phase, the broker proposed a pool structure and coverage to the study group.

While the pool was originally conceived to provide liability coverage, the study group decided to expand the coverages to include property. This would further consolidate insurance coverage in a single program and take advantage of economies of scale in both of these areas.

Structure of program

Pure self-insurance is the practice of assuming all liability without transfer to a second party. Self-insurance does not result simply from a conscious decision to stay out of the conventional marketplace, but from establishing a structured and funded program. It requires that a sum of money be appropriated annually for the purpose of paying claims. The amount set aside annually should reflect loss experience over the prior three- to five-year period. As claims are filed, they are then either paid, or reserves are set aside in anticipation of final settlement.

A self-insurance fund can be complemented with reinsurance or excess insurance policies. These policies add to the coverage offered by the self-insurance fund by indemnifying against costs of a specific nature. Two types of costs are generally involved: catastrophic losses and annual aggregate losses. In the first instance, a single large loss above a specified amount, i.e., $150,000, results in a reinsurance policy paying the difference between $150,000 and the total cost of the claim. Annual aggregate insurance protects against cumulative losses in a single policy year again in excess of a specified total, i.e., $525,000.

By combining the self-insurance fund with these two excess insurance policies, and structuring the coverage offered by the reinsurance policies so that it is identical to that offered by the pool, a "fully funded" program can be created. All possible costs and expenses associated with pool operations are paid for either by cash contribution or from the excess insurance policies purchased to complement the fund. Guarding against unanticipated expenses is critical to the smooth operation of a self-insurance plan. The costs fall in three basic areas: (1) the loss fund, (2) excess insurance, and (3) administrative services.

The CIRSA plan involves these three basic elements. First, a primary loss fund in the amount of $525,000 was established. Secondly, CIRSA purchased excess policies to cover catastrophic and annual aggregate losses. The catastrophic policy provides that a loss in excess of $150,000 will be paid from that policy. The annual aggregate policy provides that if all funds deposited in the self-insurance pool ($525,000) are spent in a single year, the annual aggregate policy will pay costs in excess of that amount. Lastly, an administrative budget was adopted to cover claims adjusting, program management, data processing, and loss prevention.

CIRSA includes a $1,000 deductible for every loss. This requirement shifts small dollar losses back to the participating municipality, although the administration, investigation, and payment of the claim is handled by the pool. This deductible reduces the cost of excess policies.

Commissioner's review

Colorado statutes provide that, prior to beginning operations, a self-insurance plan must be reviewed and approved by the insurance commissioner. This clause is designed to ensure that any self-funded plan established by Colorado municipalities is run on a sound basis consistent with prudent insurance management practices. The commissioner was contacted early in this effort and was briefed on the project's goals and objectives. He reviewed the questionnaire used to collect data and provided general guidance to the plan's development. His fundamental concerns involved experienced management and adequate funding of all costs.

When the program structure was finalized in September 1981, a formal filing was made with the commissioner. This filing included, among other documents, a complete text of the by-laws and intergovernmental agreement, specimen reinsurance policies, contracts covering plan administration, claims adjusting and banking services, an actuarial statement, and legal opinions addressing several aspects of the plan.

The commissioner's review was a constructive and valuable evaluation of the plan of operation. The commissioner and his staff pointed out necessary revisions in the by-laws to ensure that proper authority was vested in the pool's board of directors. A reinsurance carrier was deleted and replaced with a firm fully licensed to do business in Colorado.

On December 8, 1981, the commissioner issued a 30-day certificate of authority, effective January 1, 1982. The conditional certificate required the pool to undergo an examination of books, records, and facilities, as well as to submit executed documents pertaining to plan operation.

Membership enrollment

Beginning in September 1981, several meetings were held with potential pool members. Since all contact prior to this time had been with municipal staff, these meetings were with members of the governing bodies to explain the program and to request adoption of the intergovernmental contract. By late December, 19 municipalities had agreed to participate in the plan, generating approximately $1.1 million in contributions.

Plan benefits

Municipalities chose to join CIRSA because of improved insurance coverage and services offered by the pool over conventional programs.

Broader coverage Broader coverage was provided in each of the three primary insurance areas (property, general liability, and automobile). Many coverages often purchased separately, e.g., police professional, special events, and fine arts, are part of the master policy. For some communities, CIRSA membership meant coverage in 25 areas not covered by previous insurance programs. The persons insured by the pool were both consistent for each area of insurance and clearly and broadly stated to include all elected, appointed, and employed personnel.

Detailed claim reports The pool provides monthly loss reports to each participating community. The reports detail every claim filed against the community and include information concerning the person filing the claim, the nature of the claim, the cause of the accident, the amount of damages, and the amount spent to settle the claim including legal adjusting and cost award. Besides providing an historical record of losses, these reports provide a profile of loss from which to build a loss prevention program. By coding losses to reflect department and type of loss, communities can design a loss prevention program to reflect their individual needs. Cumulative data for losses incurred by the full membership is also available to assist in risk management.

Dollar savings All communities saved money by joining the pool. The average savings was approximately 30 percent, with individual savings ranging from a low of 10 percent to a high of about 50 percent. Data collected from other self-insurance programs indicate that pool costs should be relatively constant over time. Some pool programs even report a reduction in cost during the third or fourth years.

Greater control Since the pool controls by contract claims adjusting, pool members can play a more meaningful role in claims adjusting. The quality of work in this area is under the direct control of pool members, and policies concerning the settlement of certain types of claims will be established by pool members.

Loss prevention Providing a financial plan to protect against loss is merely the first element in a complete loss program. The pool will provide to members, both on an individual and collective basis, services to prevent loss and to improve safety practices. As the frequency of claims decreases, the cost of pool operations can be reduced.

Successful cooperation

By working together cooperatively, Colorado municipalities have cut costs and improved their insurance services. CIRSA will result in improved information available for making management decisions. The pool also represents a use of private sector resources that increases municipalities' ability to manage the services they pay for.

Instead of complaining about a problem while continuing to conduct "business as usual," the members of CIRSA have shown their willingness to be innovative. They have established and will no doubt improve upon a program to maximize the use and effectiveness of a precious commodity—public tax dollars.

PART 3

Special Areas of Risk

Public Officials Liability: The Loss Exposure

David J. LaBrec and Kurt Foerster

Beginning in 1978, with the U.S. Supreme Court decision in *Monell* v. *Department of Social Services of the State of New York,* municipal and public official civil rights liability has grown at an explosive rate.

This article is intended to: (1) define the civil rights exposures with which public officials, risk managers, agents, and brokers should be familiar; and (2) suggest some approaches that can be useful in dealing with these risks.

Some preliminary caveats are in order. First, although many of the principles discussed in this article relate to both public officials and entities alike, the reader should keep in mind that the courts often treat the liability of an individual official quite differently from that of the entity itself. Second, while some of the information presented here applies specifically to municipalities and municipal officials, the broader principles apply to most local governments and public officials nationwide. Third, this article is not intended as an authoritative treatise on all areas of civil rights laws, but rather focuses on some of the more common areas of exposure. Readers are urged to seek legal advice as specific cases and interpretations arise.

Civil rights (§ 1983) liability

42 U.S.C. § 1983 is the primary Civil Rights Act on which most suits against public officials and entities are based. It reads in pertinent part:

This selection is made up of two articles reprinted from the July 1984 issue of *The Risk Report* with permission of the publisher, International Risk Management Institute, Inc., Dallas, Texas.

"Every *person* who, *under color of any statute, ordinance, regulation, custom or usage,* of any state or territory . . . , *subjects, or causes to be subjected,* any citizen of the United States or other person within the jurisdiction thereof to the *deprivation of any rights, privileges, or immunities secured by the Constitution and laws,* shall be liable to the party injured in an action at law, suit inequity, or other proper proceedings for redress [emphasis added]."

Historical background Section 1983 originally came into being as Section 1 of the Ku Klux Klan Act of 1871. It was enacted in response to a request from President Grant deploring the activities of the Klan in the South. In passing the act, it was clear that Congress intended to curb the wild abandon of the Klan. For 90 years, the act was seldom used except in the protection of the right to vote, and the courts were inclined to construe narrowly the words "under color of statute, ordinance. . . . " The modern era of Section 1983 litigation began in 1961 with the United States Supreme Court decision in *Monroe* v. *Pape* in which the court held that actions of police officers in carrying out a warrantless entry and search of a private home and lengthy and abusive interrogation of the occupants constituted action "under color of law" permitting assessment of damages against the thirteen officers involved. However, the court held that the city was not a "person" which could be sued under Section 1983 and, therefore, the city itself was immune. For the next seventeen years, municipalities experienced little, if any, civil rights litigation. During that time, plaintiffs sought remedies under state law because of the difficulty of collecting monetary judgments against individual officials themselves. In 1978, after literally thousands of suits in which state and federal trial and appellate courts had held that cities were not persons under Section 1983, the United States Supreme Court reversed over a hundred years of precedent and held that municipalities were "persons" under the act and could be sued for monetary, declaratory and injunctive relief whenever the conduct of the officials implements a policy, custom, or usage of the municipality itself. The *Monell* v. *Department of Social Services of the State of New York* decision opened the door to modern civil rights lawsuits against governmental entities. A few statistics will put the effect of the *Monell* and subsequent decisions in real perspective:

1. In 1961 (the year when the *Monroe* decision was handed down), approximately 250 federal civil rights cases were pending throughout the country.
2. In 1979 (the year following the *Monell* decision), there were approximately 30,000 civil rights cases filed.
3. Civil rights suits presently comprise approximately 8 percent of the total docket of the federal courts.
4. In the 12-month period from July 1, 1982, through June 30,

1983, there were 241,842 civil rights suits filed in federal courts.

"Persons" As a result of the *Monell* decision, *both individual officials and the entities themselves are "persons" subject to liability under Section 1983.* Suits are usually brought against the entity itself and all officials who are, or could have been, in any way involved in the conduct that gave rise to the alleged civil rights violation.

Therefore, it is imperative that public officials liability insurance coverage be available to both defend and indemnify all public officials and employees who, along with the city itself, will likely be joined as defendants to such a suit.

Immunity Immunity from civil rights litigation is different for individuals and entities. *For municipalities, sovereign or governmental, immunity is virtually nonexistent* because of the 1980 Supreme Court decision in *Owen* v. *City of Independence, Missouri.* In that case, the Court held that if a civil rights violation occurs, the city is liable, even though city officials were acting in good faith belief that their actions were constitutionally permitted. A dissenting opinion by Justice Powell in the *Owen* decision suggests that cities not only are entitled to no immunity but that they are now subject to strict liability under Section 1983.

In any event, *sovereign or governmental immunity does not apply to individual officers, employees, or agents.* They have always been subject to Section 1983 liability for their own conduct.

Absolute vs. qualified immunity *Absolute immunity has uniformly been afforded to some judicial and legislative officials.* Judges at all levels, whether federal or state, are generally entitled to absolute immunity, as are prosecutors and witnesses while testifying under oath. Legislators are provided absolute immunity when acting in their legislative capacity as such.

A significant difference exists between absolute and qualified immunity. If absolute immunity applies, a suit can be dismissed at the outset, thereby saving substantial litigation expenses. Qualified immunity, on the other hand, is a defense which must be proven during the trial.

In *Harlow* v. *Fitzgerald,* the U.S. Supreme Court redefined a two-part test of qualified or "good faith" official immunity. First, if the law that the defendant is said to have violated is not clearly established at the time of the incident, then the official is entitled to dismissal from the suit. If, however, the plaintiff can show that the violated law was clear at the time of the incident, then the defendant official may establish a good faith defense by showing two things: (a) that he was not aware of the law (and, therefore, not aware of the impropriety of his actions at the time); and (b) that the average person in his situation would not have known of the law (and, therefore, the wrongfulness of the action).

Individual vs. official capacity *Individual officers and employees may be sued in either their individual or official capacity.* Civil rights actions for damages brought against defendants in their official capacities are directed against the municipality itself; that is, the relief is not sought against the individual person. Contra, a suit against a person in an individual capacity is brought against the person himself, and damages are recoverable against him personally. This distinction often becomes important where insurance coverage provides protection only for officials when acting in their official capacity.

Damages Some concrete examples of these loss exposures include: (a) a $3.5 million judgment which effectively bankrupted the town of South Tucson, Arizona; (b) a $1.4 million judgment against the city of Borger, Texas, and individual officers for the shooting of an innocent party during the late night apprehension of a known felon; (c) a $1 million suit against the city of Ennis, Texas (population 12,110), by a man who claimed that he was unlawfully jailed for violating the city animal leash ordinance; and (d) a multimillion dollar suit against the city of Stanton, California, by a police officer alleging that the city was negligent in failing to properly train him, resulting in his shooting of a citizen.

These examples obviate the diverse theories under which Section 1983 actions are developed. Two conclusions can be drawn. First, never assume that the amount of damages asserted in a civil rights action is directly related to the nature or extent of the alleged wrong. Second, be mindful that the theories used to develop these actions are limited only by the imaginations of plaintiffs and the lawyers who represent them.

Punitive damages In *Fact Concerts, Inc.* v. *City of Newport* (1981), the U.S. Supreme Court was confronted with the question of whether municipalities themselves may be held liable for punitive damages in Section 1983 actions and, to the surprise of many, the question was answered in the negative. *At present, the punitive damage immunity of municipalities remains intact. However, no such immunity exists for officials sued in their individual capacities.*

Pendent state claims Civil rights suits may be brought in federal or state courts. Those brought in state courts are brought as pendent actions, in conjunction with actions under state law. In Texas, for example, civil rights actions were often brought in conjunction with suits arising under the Texas Tort Claims Act. Many defenses and immunities can be asserted in state court which might not otherwise be available if the action were brought in federal court. For example, under Texas law, governmental immunity exists for any conduct involving the "method or manner of providing police protection." A suit brought in state court alleging police misconduct can, therefore, be successfully defended and, hopefully, dismissed, and the pendent Section 1983 cause of action can be dismissed along with it. Additionally, joint and several liability of the defendants often exists under state laws but, in a federal civil rights action, the liability of the individual and the municipality are quite different.

On the other hand, civil rights suits filed in federal court are often accompanied by a pendent state court claim. One reason for bringing an action in federal court can be to avoid state comparative negligence laws which can reduce the amount of recoverable damages.

Indemnity In many jurisdictions, *it is illegal for the municipality to indemnify an official or employee sued in his or her individual capacity and, in some states, no authority exists even to spend public funds to defend public employees and officials.* If liability insurance

Public official liability questions

Salvatore Perillo, County Counsel for Atlantic County, New Jersey, presents below a number of excellent questions that municipal officials should be asking their insurance agents regarding the extent of their public officials liability coverage.

1. Are we (our government and the individual public officials) covered for civil rights claims under 42 USC 1983? Punitive damages? Opposing parties counsel fees?
2. Are we covered for damages as a result of inverse condemnation action? Cost of defense? Opposing parties counsel fees?
3. Are we covered for environmental impairment liability (E.I.L.)? Are there any exclusions? "Pre-existing condition" exclusion? Solid waste landfill; incinerator, etc.?
4. Are the activities of our attorneys, engineers, planners, accountants, physicians covered?
5. Do we have any right to approve settlements? Is this right unconditional or qualified?
6. Can our deductible be applied to our carrier's cost of defense?
7. Do we have the right to approve (or veto) choice of counsel?

GRMR adds one additional question:

8. Is your coverage on a "pay on behalf of" or "indemnity" form?

Source: *Governmental Risk Management Reports*, July 1983, a monthly periodical published by Risk Planning Group, division of Tillinghast, Nelson and Warren, Inc.

does not provide defense and indemnification, those officials and employees who are sued must face the reality of using their own funds to defend themselves. This often leads to discord among defendants that enhances the plaintiff's likelihood of recovery.

General principles Liability does not arise for municipalities and officials by the mere fact that a subordinate officer or employee caused a constitutional deprivation. There must be shown a nexus between the conduct which caused the deprivation or there must be proof of a generally accepted city policy condoning the unconstitutional conduct.

Generally, a sole incident is insufficient to establish a custom, policy, or usage sufficient to give rise to a cause of action under Section 1983.

The "rights" protected under Section 1983 include rights under the Constitution itself and also purely statutory violations of federal law.

Attorneys' fees The Civil Rights Attorneys' Fee Act of 1976 (42 USC § 1988) provides in part:

> ... In any action or proceeding to enforce a provision of ... Section 1983 ... the Court, in its discretion, may allow the prevailing party ... a reasonable attorneys fee as part of the cost.

The courts have interpreted "prevailing party" differently for plaintiffs than they have for defendants. In fact, a plaintiff may be considered a prevailing party even under circumstances where the case is settled out of court prior to a trial. On the other hand, for defendants to recover their costs, it must generally be shown that the plaintiff's suit was totally without merit, frivolous, unreasonable or without foundation. The likelihood that a defendant will recover attorneys' fees in a civil rights action (even if he is successful in defending it) is remote. Thus, *it is important that public officials liability insurance coverages include provisions for defense as well as payment of plaintiff's attorneys' fees and costs of court.*

Conclusion Public officials liability will continue to be a major risk management challenge for municipalities in the future. Risk managers and insurance representatives must take positive steps toward handling this exposure before presented with a suit.

Public officials liability insurance

Lawsuits and judgments against municipalities and elected officials have increased geometrically over the last few years. Broad interpretations have also expanded remedies allowed by federal law (under 42 USC 1981 *et seq.*). In key cases since *Monell,* the "vicarious liability" of the elected official and employee has been extended into unexpected areas. For example, is a judgment under 42 USC 1988 (plaintiff's attorneys' fees) against a judge for issuing an erroneous bench warrant a step towards the erosion of judicial immunity? Two cases like this have occurred in Virginia alone.

This, coupled with the erosion of sovereign immunity, state "tort acts," federal pleadings, and an aggressive plaintiff's bar has created a critical need for quality public officials liability (POL) coverage.

General information POL may be one of the broadest liability insurance coverages written. The POL policy covers "wrongful acts," excluding bodily injury, property damage, and personal injury, which are covered under a CGL form. Examples of "wrongful acts" are shown in Exhibit 1. The ultimate purpose of the POL policy is to protect the taxpayers' money and the individual officials' and employees' personal assets.

Policy features POL forms are difficult to compare and, because the POL policy has been in the marketplace only since the mid-1970's, there are few court interpretations of policy language. However, there are several commonly worded exclusions found in most policies. (When in doubt about any interpretation, ask the underwriter and, of course, get it in writing.)

The policy checklist, Exhibit 2, will provide assistance in mak-

Dismissal of employee	Failure to disclose information
Failure to follow legal procedures	Failure to examine documents
Failure to provide service	Failure to supervise employees
Disciplinary actions—employees	Permitting misuse of information
Employee hiring	Permitting unauthorized payments
Zoning/permits	Improper bidding
Promotion/tenure	Failure to use finance opportunities
Labor negotiations	Failure to detect a crime
Issuance of licenses	Failure to obtain insurance
Service quality	Improper reimbursements
Title 7 discrimination	Actions beyond powers of office
Conduct of inspections	Discrimination (1983, *et al.*)
Purchasing of goods/services	Antitrust
Administration of grants	Subsequent unconstitutional acts
Transportation/livery	Conflict with federal law
Sale of land	Improper expansion planning
Property condemnation	Project-expansion overruns
Annexation/detachment	Eminent domain
Failure to attend functions	Frivolous suits, *i.e.*, defense cost
Silence on other's improprieties	Noise abatement standards
Incur unnecessary expenses	Space allocation

Exhibit 1. Public official liability exposures.

ing comparisons. One should find lower cost with less coverage, but this is not necessarily true in the current marketplace. A quick review of the policy features follows.

"Claims-made" versus occurrence form Most policies are on a claims-made basis, allowing the insurer to avoid the "long tail" associated with most professional liability claims. The advantage of an occurrence form, assuming broad coverage and adequate limits, is that the policy period is covered forever.

Since the date of loss is difficult to determine in many cases (as in faulty inspections, cost cutting on projects, environmental contamination, etc.), for a growing community that has not had POL coverage before, a true claims-made form may offer the most affordable coverage for any unknown/undiscovered claims. Because of the advantages to both parties, the claims-made forms are generally more readily available. A *limited* claims-made form will have a "retro" cut-off date to limit prior acts to two or three years.

Keep in mind the pitfalls of converting from a "claims-made" to an "occurrence" policy (i.e., cutting off the "tail" coverage). Only do it when broad prior acts coverage is available, with as many years retro as can be obtained.

"Pay on behalf" versus "indemnify the insured" Most policies now "pay on behalf." The "indemnifying" policy leaves a client to his

- Covered "wrongful acts"
- Claims-made policy
- Occurrence basis policy (are you converting from "claims-made"?)
- Pay on behalf of type policy
- All officials, past, present, and future
- All employees and volunteers
- All civil rights violations (42 USC 1981 *et seq.*)
- 60 day notice of cancellation
- Guaranteed policy extension, 36 months, even if insured cancels 30 day notice to take "discovery period" option
- Antitrust-type suits
- Punitive and exemplary damages
- All discrimination suits covered
- Zoning suits covered
- Sudden and accidental pollution
- Advertising, broadcasting, telecasting
- Limited fiduciary roles exclusions
- Attorneys, engineers, accountants, and architects (if employees) covered
- Prior acts (limitations? retro dates?)
- Expert municipal defense attorneys
- Defense cost beyond policy limits
- Defense costs for injunctive relief suits covered
- No stacking deductibles (per loss)
- Endorsements by associations (related to your entity)
- Other risk management services (info, mailings, loss control, etc.)
- "A"-rated insurance carriers (B+XII) or less—get cut-through endorsement)
- Admitted carriers
- Approved surplus lines carrier

Exhibit 2. POL policy checklist.

own defense (at times, an error on the insurer's part) and without confirmation of coverage until it is time for *reimbursement*.

"Broad" insured definitions Definition should include past, present, future officials, all employees, and volunteers. Most POL forms exclude coverage for schools, airports, electric/gas utilities, public transportation, and hospitals. Usually, these can be deleted, depending on the exposure, for a charge.

Note that separate POL forms for those operations/authorities (e.g., school boards) may be advisable. In these times of fiscal restraint, the school board may be forced to file suit against the local government over budgeting practices. Remember that, with several entities on the same policy, the various entities' losses are subject to the same annual aggregate. There is also a possibility of conflict on the choice of counsel with the same carrier involved.

Civil rights (state/federal coverage) Coverage for 42 USC 1981 *et seq.* (especially 1983, 1985, 1986, 1988) is critical since it will be the basis of many suits. Sections 1983 and 1988 are summarized in the preceding article.

Exclusions Exclusions in the various policies vary substantially. Thorough analysis of the exclusionary language is critical when reviewing and comparing policies. Some standard exclusions include:

1. Gaining profit or advantages not allowed by law
2. Fraud and/or dishonesty, but not for the innocent also named in the suit
3. Losses covered by other valid policies (i.e., CGL, BAP, PI)
4. Bodily injury, property damage, personal injury (direct or consequential)
5. Pollution, contamination, and radiation
6. Claims which should have been reported to the previous carrier
7. Injunctive relief
8. Inverse condemnation/adverse possession/dedication by adverse use
9. Fiduciary responsibility arising out of ERISA/self-insurance plans
10. Contractual penalties
11. Voluntary refunds of monies.

There are also other exclusions that are found in some insurers' forms and not others. The deletion of these exclusions is frequently negotiable if they are in a particular form. They include:

1. Law enforcement operations/agencies;

2. Contractual;
3. Maintaining insurance;
4. Cost estimate overruns/faulty planning;
5. Improper use of funds;
6. Failure to supply water/power;
7. Punitive damages; and
8. Civil rights/EEOC/Title 7/past wages due/statutory penalties.

Cancellation Most forms currently offer 30-day notice of cancellation. An attempt to amend this provision to 60 days and, in some instances, 90 days will often prove fruitful. For the risk with an adverse loss ratio, a lot of work is necessary to replace coverage and this extra time may be needed.

Defense cost beyond limits Since few suits filed actually result in an award, defense costs coverage that does not impact the annual aggregate is extremely desirable. Defense costs for these claims can be extremely high.

Punitive and exemplary damages Reviews of states allowing punitive damages to be awarded and insured, contained in various publications, are not consistent. A decision from local counsel is appropriate in this area. Should the state allow coverage, purchase it. Also, beware of the literal interpretation states where silence does not afford coverage.

Extended discovery period extension The discovery period extends the time to report claims first made during the policy period, with options from one to three years. The cost of the option varies. This exercise of the discovery period is very important if the insured ever wishes to *convert* to an occurrence form. A rarity in the marketplace is an option to exercise the discovery period when the *insured cancels* or does not renew. Most policies at this time will only allow the purchase of the discovery period if the *company cancels* or nonrenews.

Reporting period for claims Some claims-made policies allow one year to report claims to the company for claims made against the insured during the policy period. Not all policies have this; most claims-made policies require that the claim must be made during the policy period and reported to the company during the policy period.

Other areas of available coverage Antitrust, zoning disputes, limited fiduciary, sudden/accidental pollution, advertising/broadcasting/telecasting, coverage for attorneys and architects/engineers, unlimited prior acts for unknown/undiscovered wrongful acts, defense of injunctive relief, per loss deductibles, are widely available and extremely desirable features.

Claims practices Expect a reservation of rights letter about 75% of the time. The problem is that the allegations will have to get "boiled down," usually before trial, and that the POL form is not the policy of "last resort." A defense attorney should be designated early; avoid waiting until a suit is filed. Most carriers are willing to work with a qualified staff attorney on small claims.

Reducing the Threat of Personal and Administrative Liability

John C. Pine

Public officials and administrators in increasing numbers are finding that they are involved in tort liability suits individually and as representatives of governmental units.[1]

In Louisiana, the State Constitution allows suits against the state.[2] As a result, neither the state, state agencies, nor political subdivisions are immune from suits. A citizen in the state of Louisiana may bring suit against a public official or the public jurisdiction if the citizen believes damages have resulted from the actions of the officers or employees of the public jurisdiction. The Louisiana Civil Code provides an avenue for a citizen to seek redress from the individual governmental official for acts that cause damage to others. Under the civil code each person is obliged to repair damages caused to others.[3] The governmental jurisdiction may also be vicariously responsible for the actions of their employees.[4]

In addition to liability under Louisiana law, individual officers and local jurisdictions may also be sued under Section 1983 of the Civil Rights Act for damages resulting from deprivations of citizen rights, privileges, or immunities secured by the United States Constitution and federal laws.[5] From 1961 to 1974, the number of private civil rights filings in federal courts increased from 296 cases to 8,159 cases, an increase of more than 2,700%. By 1979 the number had increased to 16,849 cases, an increase of 106% over 1974 filings.

In response to the threat of personal liability suits, some public officials refuse to continue to hold public office, as in the case of the

Reprinted with permission from the January-February 1983 issue of the *Louisiana Municipal Review*, published by the Louisiana Municipal Association.

former mayor of Greenville, Mississippi, who quit after twelve years of public service. The mayor cited problems of personal liability, especially under Section 1983, as the reason many officials are saying, "I am not going to run and subject myself to this."[6] The elected officials of a small Kansas town had a healthy respect for the threat of liability and sought protection through liability insurance. They found that the premium exceeded the total town budget. They voted to disband the town.[7]

The possibility of a suit against a public official or the jurisdiction is not an idle threat. One governmental jurisdiction in Louisiana has been required to pay judgments of more than $1.6 million within a one-year period.[8] The question facing public officials today is how this liability exposure can be managed so that it does not interfere with official actions and the administration of public jurisdictions.

Potential liability for the individual public official and the governmental jurisdiction is real and may dampen state and local government's enthusiasm for taking innovative approaches toward program management.[9] It is apparent that as public officials exercise their discretion, the probability of a court challenge of their administration of city programs and services increases. Given that citizens are more likely to challenge administrative actions in the future, there are actions that public administrators and officials can take to reduce the threat of liability so that financial resources can be used to provide public services rather than compensation for damages caused by public employees and their agencies. It will be suggested here that managers and public officials can act now to prevent, reduce, or eliminate the risk of liability personally and organizationally. This article will not provide a legal defense to liability suits but will outline some administrative actions that public officials can take to prevent damage from occurring.

What can be done?

In attacking complex and difficult problems, we look for alternatives that provide immediate relief. Changing state and federal laws to limit the liability of individual officers and organizations would offer immediate relief; however, the legislative process is time consuming and the results are not always predictable. Transferring the risk of a liability judgment to an insurance company, or to an insurance pool, does allow a jurisdiction to minimize financial loss, but neither of these strategies solves the problem of actions by employees, officers, or the organization, which can also be the basis for damage suits by citizens or even employees. An effective program to confront and deal with the threat of liability should involve not only shifting the risk but also taking systematic steps to (1) identify potential risks, hazards and exposure to liability; (2) implement a program to reduce the possibility of loss; and (3) monitor the activities of the governmental jurisdiction to control for loss.

The fundamental principles of law also make sound management principles.[10] Throughout the cases imposing personal and organizational liability for civil rights violations and liability to cities under the Louisiana Civil Code is a common thread of administrative mistakes, such as a lack of supervision of employees, or poorly conceived to nonexistent administrative procedures. Conversely, the antidotes to personal liability and liability of parishes and cities are clearly defined procedures, drafted with an eye toward protecting the rights of individuals and well-trained and supervised personnel who are themselves accorded fair treatment. Maintaining a scrupulous respect for the constitutional rights of others in the performance of public duties may not always be an easy rule to observe, but it is essential in avoiding litigation. A famous judicial quotation, speaking to the scope of a municipality's duty to repair streets, states that a "drunken man is as much entitled to a safe street as a sober one, and much more in need of it."[11] The same might be said for the constitutional rights of all persons, be their behavior objectionable or not, to enjoy their rights of free speech, privacy, security of person and property and freedom from arbitrary governmental action.

As a result of damage awards paid by public officials and agencies for violations of constitutional rights and statutory protections, public agency officials at the state and local level must recognize the importance of a new standard for administrative practice.[12] Increased accountability through the courts establishes a balance between the needs of the individual and those of the administrative state by requiring public administrators to be cognizant of the constitutional and legal rights of private individuals before acting upon them.

Identifying potential exposure

Many public officials contend that it is unreasonable for a city to be held liable for an injury caused by a dangerous condition that has not been reported. However, the law holds that government is accountable. Management is being forced to make a concentrated effort to identify potential liability by analyzing those services that pose the greatest risk. By reviewing accident reports, public officials may be able to prevent accidents and losses. Judgments against other governmental units may indicate potential problems for a jurisdiction. In suits involving negligence of public officials and employees, failure to take reasonable steps to prevent injury has been claimed by plaintiffs seeking damages. In one slip-and-fall incident in a city recreation facility, the public agency had received complaints of slippery concrete floors but only partially attempted to remove the hazard.[13] Complaints had been made to management concerning slippery floors throughout the facility but mats were placed only in the women's restroom. A citizen using the recreation facility slipped on a wet floor and sued the city stating that the wet floor posed a dangerous condition. The court ruled that the proprietor has a duty of reasonable care which included the prior discovery of unreasonably dangerous conditions and a duty to warn users. The testimony during the trial indicated a general awareness by employees of the slippery condition throughout the facility, not just in the women's restroom. The injured woman was trying to be careful but still slipped on the wet concrete floor.

The courts are not requiring an unreasonable standard of care for government to anticipate every possible hazard. In a personal injury suit against a school board, the parents of a seventh-grade student sued claiming negligence when their son was hurt in a fight. The court stated that the school personnel did everything reasonably possible to prevent the altercation but could not do so and thus the evidence was not sufficient to sustain the finding of liability on the part of the school board or school personnel. A greater degree of care is required when an object or activity is inherently dangerous, that is, when it is *reasonably foreseeable* that an accident could occur. The school personnel had no reason to anticipate a fight and thus no duty to guard the students.[14]

Agency personnel may wish to work with national professional associations to clarify or develop standards of professional practice. Public works, building codes, fire, police, finance and personnel officials' associations can provide assistance in clarifying professional standards.

Periodic inspections or preventive maintenance should be made in areas that could lead to liability suits. The financial savings of implementing a preventive liability program are far greater than responding to charges in court, even if liability damages are not awarded against the governmental jurisdiction. An incentive program can be carried out to identify hazards. Employees may be rewarded for reporting the absence of a stop sign. Garbage workers on at least a weekly basis cover the city and could notice potential hazards; police in their normal patrols also have frequent opportunities to notice hazards that could lead to liability for the governmental jurisdiction.

Reducing risk

Every jurisdiction should develop comprehensive policies and procedures for its activities. Informed, well-trained employees following specified work procedures may reduce costly judgments. In a suit against a local jurisdiction contesting the city's dismissal of a police officer, the court cited the city's personnel policies as a determining factor in the case. Liability was not assessed against the city when a police officer was terminated for violating a rule prohibiting drinking in a bar while on sick leave. The city had provided notice to the employee by warnings and progressive disciplinary actions that such off-duty conduct would diminish public confidence in the police force. The officer had been warned not to return to the lounge. By using progressive disciplinary actions the city provided due process and was able to avoid liability.[15]

The presence of clear rules for employee conduct provided the basis for liability when a doctor employed by a state agency refused to treat a prison inmate and then confined the inmate to a cell for nine days. The action by the doctor was in violation of a department rule that stated that medical attention must be given to inmates. Damages of $2,500 were assessed against the doctor for the manner in which the inmate was confined and for failure to comply with the agency regulation.[16]

Caution must be exercised, however, because the employer may still be vicariously liable even when an employee clearly fails to comply with stated policies and procedures. For example, an employer was liable for the damage caused by a fire even though an employee was specially instructed not to burn trash, the action which caused the fire.[17] Generally speaking, an employee is expected to adhere to the employer's rules and regulations and his failure to do so may under certain circumstances negate vicarious liability on the part of the employer. However, the court may view the employee's actions as within the scope of employment even though the employee's conduct was contrary to his employer's expressed direction, rules or wishes.[18] The test of the employer's responsibility for the acts of an employee is not whether the act was done in accordance with the rules, but whether the employee's actions were part of the job. An act is regarded as "authorized" in the legal sense if it is incidental to the performance of the duties entrusted to the employee even though it is in disobedience of the employer's expressed orders and instructions.[19] A final factor in determining whether the employer may be responsible for the actions of the employee is whether the employee's actions were substantially within the authorized limits of time and space and were undertaken in part with the intent to serve the employer.[20]

Although policies, procedures and instructions may not provide an effective defense for vicarious liability for the employee's actions, they do give employees clear direction to guide their behavior in avoiding problems for themselves and the agency. Clear instructions and established procedures are likely to lead to the type of employee behavior that does no harm to others. Clear guidelines reduce the risk of an employee not knowing how to proceed or when to act or what the agency would like the employee to do. The agency can emphasize in memos, signs, posters, etc., that "these are public records," "under these conditions, do not mow," political campaigning is forbidden or that procedures must be followed when purchasing for the agency.

Training for employees and management personnel on agency policies and procedures helps to avoid negligent acts and mistakes made from ignorance of correct procedures and policies. Employees who realize potential legal consequences of their actions will likely comply with the agency rules. Training in critical incidents can help employees understand how to respond and avoid liability for themselves and the agency. One public agency was considered liable when a bus driver encouraged a rider to commit a violent act against a person. The court considered the bus driver's actions within the scope of his employment. The court determined that the employee was performing some functions for his employer that he was employed to do when the violent incident occurred. Effective training could have helped the bus driver understand his own reaction to the pressures of the situation and respond more effectively. If an employee has a confusing problem on the job, clear instructions on who to call and how to respond could have eliminated the hassles of court proceedings and damages assessed against the public agency.[21] Employees who are subjected to extensive pressures might be screened more extensively in employment interviews. Finally, simulations of work situations could test the applicants' ability to handle high-pressure situations.

Prompt, careful attention to duties can eliminate awards for simple negligence by employees. An employer was held to be negligent for failing to notify an employee of a serious medical condition discovered in a pre-employment physical required by the employer. The employee learned of the employer's negligence after she sought medical attention for a chronic cough. The examining physician reviewed her record and informed her of the results of the pre-employment physical that had revealed tuberculosis.[22]

Public officials can gain the cooperation of employees in avoiding liability when they explain the liability of the individual employees and the agency. For example, damages were assessed against a public employee when the court determined that the employee was acting outside the scope of his employment. The court also found that the employer was negligent.[23]

There is no better way of reducing the risk of liability than to provide for the immediate repair of unsafe conditions that may result in an accident. In one case, the court determined that the agency had notice of the unsafe condition of a road for years and assessed damages against the agency.[24] In another case, an agency was held liable for failure to maintain a highway when a pothole was the cause of an accident.[25] "The agency knew or should have known that the roadway was in a defective condition," the court said. The agency failed to warn of an unsafe condition and failed to monitor the condition of the road.

The private sector has stressed the involvement of both management and employees in reducing risks and liability for many years. Reviewing how flammable chemicals, poison and dangerous equipment are stored can prevent injuries to persons who do not realize the potential hazards. Safety inspections by professionals in code enforcement, fire, police, or the city engineer's office could identify potential dangers. Action to eliminate risks should be taken now; waiting will only increase the possibility of potential damages.

Controlling potential risks

Supervisors and foremen should understand the importance of monitoring employee actions on the job. Management must ensure that supervisors and employees comply with directives. The failure to monitor and supervise employees resulted in damages against an agency when, despite the directions of the district manager, "Ice on the Bridge" signs were not displayed when the weather service declared a freeze warning in central Louisiana. Despite his careful efforts, the driver lost control of his car on an icy bridge and sued the agency for failure to warn of the unsafe condition. Failure to monitor the employee's behavior proved to be a costly error to the agency. In another case the court decided that the school officials failed to provide adequate supervision when a child was injured by a protruding screw while sliding down a pole.[26]

A final method of controlling for risks is to conduct an audit of personnel policies and procedures to ensure compliance with constitutional rights and statutory provisions. Awards of back pay are just as costly as awards for damages when employees make mistakes while conducting the public's business. For example, many dismissals must be for cause and charges must be proven.[27]

Conclusion

Actions by public officials and employees that are in line with normal professional practices are likely to be viewed by the courts as valid actions and not misfeasance. In a recent case the court held that employees of a police jury had done a "professional job" in dredging a canal and that they had not contributed to the deterioration of a home located near the recently dredged canal. The court said the actions of the police jury in dredging the canal were appropriate and met professional standards of practice.[28]

In strict liability suits where knowledge of an unreasonable hazard or risk is not required for an award of damages, the only strategy for a public agency is to try to anticipate and identify potential risks through strict preventive maintenance programs. In suits of negligence, it is the governmental unit's duty to protect the public that has been breached. Professional practices, training, supervision and monitoring employee actions can minimize and even eliminate damages resulting from negligence. In suits involving violation of constitutional or statutory rights, management must develop clear policies and procedures and ensure that employees carry them out. A respect for the rights of citizens, clients and employees is essential to an acceptable standard of practice under the law and to good management practice.

A pervasive question in any discussion of the threat of the liability of public employees, officials and employers is whether the threat of individual or organizational liability interferes with the management of local government. The answer is yes if public officials and employees perceive that they are unable to do anything to anticipate or prevent a citizen from being damaged. However, the threat of liability does not interfere in the ongoing activities of local government if each public employee and governmental official perceives that actions can be taken to manage the affairs of the public agency in such a way as to:

1. Identify hazards and potential risks
2. Take actions to reduce these risks
3. Control and monitor actions of public employees to prevent harm to others.

These recommendations require immediate action, with long-term results and implications. As governments develop good policies and procedures, effectively train employees and monitor results of work, the public will be served more effectively and, at the same time, the risk of liability will be reduced. Liability of local governmental units under the Louisiana Constitution, Civil Code, and under 42 USC 1983 is holding government to a greater degree of accountability. At the same time, increased public liability may encourage government to provide more effective services and to manage better because of that threat.

1. "Why More Bureaucrats Are Being Sued," *U.S. News and World Report*, September 8, 1980, p. 44.
2. Constitution of the state of Louisiana (January 1, 1975), Art. 12, sec. 10.
3. Louisiana Civil Code, secs. 2315-2317.
4. Louisiana Civil Code, secs. 2320, 2324.
5. 42 USC Section 1983.
6. "Surprising Trend: You Can Beat City Hall," *U.S. News and World Report*, August 8, 1977, p. 67.
7. Mashaw, "Discussion of Civil Liability of Government Officials," 42 Law and Contemporary Problems, 80, 1978.
8. "Local Government Looking for Solution to Liability Dilemma," Baton Rouge *State-Times*, May 19, 1981.
9. W. S. Groszyk and T. J. Madden, "Managing Without Immunity: The Challenge of State and Local Officials in the 1980s," *Public Administration Review*, March-April, 1981.
10. Charles McManis, "Personal Liability of Public Officials," *Georgia Law*

Review, Vol. 9 (1976), 821.
11. McManis, p. 826.
12. D. Rosenbloom, "Public Administrators Official Immunity and the Supreme Court: Developments During the 1970's," *Public Administration Review*, March–April, 1980.
13. *Jones* v. *Recreation and Parks Commission of East Baton Rouge*, 395 So. 2d. 846, La. Ct. App., 1st Cir., 1980.
14. *Harris* v. *Bogalusa City School Board*, 393 So. 2d. 751, La. Ct. App., 1st Cir., 1980.
15. *Timmons* v. *Municipal Fire and Police Civil Service Board of Bogalusa*, 389 So. 2d. 410, La. App., 2nd Cir., 1980.
16. *State* v. *Brown*, 393 So. 2d. 113, La. Ct. App., 1st Cir., 1980.
17. *Poydras* v. *Parker*, 392 So. 2d. 94, La. Ct. of App., 1st Cir., 1980.
18. *Norman* v. *City of New Orleans*, 363 So. 2d. 1220, La. App., 4th Cir., 1978.
19. *Bordelo* v. *Great American Indemnity Co.*, 124 So. 2d. 634, La. App., 3rd Cir., 1960.
20. William L. Prosser, *Handbook on the Law of Torts*, 4th ed. (St. Paul, Minn.: West Publishing Co., 1971).
21. *Wesysham* v. *New Orleans Public Service, Inc.*, 385 So. 2d. 19, La. App., 4th Cir., 1981.
22. *Dornak* v. *Lafayette General Hospital*, 389 So. 2d. 168, Sup. Ct. La., 1981.
23. *Daniels* v. *Comm*, Supp. 382 So. 2d. 94–5, Sup. Ct. of La., 1980.
24. *Acosta* v. *State of Louisiana*, 399 So. 2d. 1189, La. App., 4th Cir., 1981.
25. *Scott* v. *State Department of Transportation and Development*, 392 So. 2d. 482, La. App., 1st Cir., 1980.
26. *Gibbons* v. *Orleans Parish School Board*, 391 So. 2d. 976, La. Ct. App., 4th Cir., 1980.
27. *Albert* v. *Louisiana State Penitentiary*, 396 So. 2d. 340, La. App., 1st Cir., 1981.
28. *Terrebonne Parish Police Jury* v. *Matherne*, 394 So. 2d. 1302, La. Ct. App., 1st Cir., 1981.

Officer Survival Recommendations: New Civil Liability Concerns

Robert W. Wennerholm

The young police officer had been on the force for three years when he responded to a burglary in progress. Two armed youths emerged from a warehouse window as the squad car stopped. There were a number of shots fired by the officer and the burglars. After two days in the hospital, the officer died. There was a large funeral. Officers from three states attended. A plaque was installed in the headquarters of the police department and the young widow received the posthumously awarded medal.

Two months later, the widow filed a law suit accusing the agency of causing her husband's death through poor training and supervision. The police chief and his top aides were all named personally. The widow asked for $10 million from the agency and $1 million each from the chief and his top staff.

No, that scenario has not yet occurred, nor have I heard of a law suit with those facts. In most cases where an officer is killed or severely injured in the line of duty, there is no thought of filing a law suit directly against the agency or its chief. Everyone assumes that officers are well-trained and that their death or serious injury is unrelated to the training or supervision provided by the department.

But things are beginning to change. It's been reported that a number of police officers on the West Coast have been changing their wills, adding a direction to the executor to institute a law suit against the chief and the department if they are killed in the line of

Reproduced from *The Police Chief* magazine, June 1984 issue, with permission of the International Association of Chiefs of Police, 13 Firstfield Road, Gaithersburg, Maryland 20878.

duty. Their concern is substandard training. They feel poorly prepared for the increasing dangers of the street.

While the death of an officer may be the most tragic aspect of police work, its monetary impact on a department is relatively small. If the agency and its personnel appear to have acted responsibly during a fatal incident, the insurance claims are filed and a fixed death benefit is paid. The dead officer cannot testify that the department's lack of training contributed to his death.

In a case of severe injury, however, where an officer is left a quadraplegic, the monetary exposure of the department can be astronomical. The actual damages involved in the care of a medically disabled worker can run into hundreds of thousands of dollars per year to provide 24-hour-a-day care. Just the sight of a previously vigorous young police officer reduced to a wheelchair can evoke million-dollar judgments for pain and suffering. Additionally, the officer can be a persuasive witness regarding the level of training and supervision he received.

S. Tucson avoids bankruptcy

The city of South Tucson—which had considered filing for bankruptcy as a result of a $3.6 million lawsuit—has reached a settlement with Roy Garcia, the former Tucson police officer who brought suit against the tiny community.

Garcia became paralyzed from the waist down after being accidentally shot by a South Tucson police officer. The incident occurred while both men were involved in a police siege of a shotgun-wielding man barricaded inside a house in South Tucson. At that time, South Tucson had a mutual aid agreement with Tucson.

In 1980, a Pima County Superior Court jury ordered South Tucson to pay Garcia $3.6 million. South Tucson, which had only $100,000 in liability insurance when the October 1978 siege took place, appealed the decision. However, the decision was upheld by the state supreme court, and the federal court declined to review the case because it did not involve federal law.

The city had considered filing for bankruptcy in response to the judgment, which was 1.5 times bigger than its annual budget. However, in November 1984, the South Tucson city council approved the sale of $2.1 million in special revenue bonds, the proceeds from which will go to Garcia. According to the newsletter *Risk Line,* "the city, rather than selling the bonds itself, formed a municipal property corporation to obtain a better credit rating. The bonds will be sold through the corporation to a Massachusetts company, and then the corporation will make a single payment to the city."

Under terms of the agreement reached with Garcia, the city is to pay Garcia $2.6 million in cash and property.

Source: March 1985 PRIMALETTER.

New survival research

In the past few years, a number of detailed research studies have focused on police officer survival. A large number of incidents where police officers were injured or killed have been analyzed.[1] Two areas that have been central in causing the injuries and deaths are unsafe tactics and techniques.

"Tactics" generally refers to the officer's response to a situation, such as investigating a disturbance, arresting a criminal, or searching an area. In an arrest situation, the tactical goal is to place the subject in custody with minimal injury to the criminal, innocent citizens, and the police officers. Safety is always a primary consideration in tactics.

Police techniques involve the use of weapons, including hands, sticks, chemicals, and firearms, in achieving tactical goals. Effective techniques allow the officer to apply force in a controlled manner while accomplishing the tactical goal of arresting the suspect and protecting innocent citizens and himself.

Too often in the past, officers have had little tactical training and have seldom considered it of value. In a previous era, a larger percentage of anti-social citizens and hardened criminals would react submissively to the mere presence of police officers. There was less need to react aggressively. There were also fewer firearms and other weapons in the hands of the criminal population. When most arrestees presented no threat, there was little need to study tactics and techniques in depth.

But times have changed. Criminals have become more aggressive and aware of their own tactical needs, a greater percentage of the non-criminal population has become emotionally unstable, and the number of weapons in society has increased dramatically. As a result, assaults on police officers have risen in the past 10 years at a geometric rate.

The research has shown that many officers exhibit the "John Wayne Syndrome," approaching a suspect or crime location without any concern for cover or adequate backup personnel. They are often at a tactical disadvantage whenever the unexpected occurs.

The result has been an increase in injuries to officers and innocent citizens. An unknown result may be fewer arrests. Officers who sense that they are unprepared to handle potentially dangerous situations will be less aggressive.

Recommended changes

Based on an analysis of the research, new tactics and techniques have been proposed. They are embodied in a number of recent books and periodicals.[2]

Tactical recommendations include an emphasis on planning, cover, and an adequate use of support personnel. The new techniques in firearm handling include an emphasis on such skills as rapidly drawing and firing within short time frames at multiple targets under various lighting conditions, reloading from various positions, clearing malfunctions, and using various supports.

Both Charles Remsberg, one of the authors of *Street Survival,* and William Rogers, a police training instructor at Jacksonville, Fla., advocate significant changes from the tactics and techniques presently used in a majority of police agencies. Their methods of training are also different from those practiced by most agencies.

Implicit in their writings and comments is a significant change in the supervisory expectations of most departments. They have not dealt directly with supervisory responsibilities, but the implications are clear. If tactics and techniques must be improved, then supervision must also be upgraded.

It appears that such commentators are attempting to raise the standards of police tactics and techniques. Their concepts should increase the level of efficiency in police work, though that may not be a sufficient reason for adopting their recommendations.

If their recommendations dramatically increase the safety standards for police work, however, police chiefs who continue to maintain old and unsafe procedures will become much more vulnerable to law suits.

Duty of agency and management

A police department exists to provide protection to the citizens. Since criminal activity is generally accomplished by the use of force, the officer must be given adequate skills, support, and equipment to encounter that force in a safe manner. Force must be used to overcome the criminal who, when confronted by the police, would either continue the crime or flee the scene.

When an agency sets up tasks that involve danger to its own employees or to third parties, it has a duty to take all reasonable steps to minimize the danger. In the case of police work, a responsibility is created to three significant groups: innocent citizens, arrestees, and employees of the agency.

Whenever a dangerous, armed individual resists arrest, a potential danger exists and force, including the use of firearms, may be necessary. It is the agency's duty to minimize the danger, within the limitations of the available equipment, tactics, and techniques. An analogy would be in the area of motor vehicles used by officers.

In the early days of automotive design, all vehicles were equipped with mechanical brakes. When the mechanical brake was the standard of the industry, an agency or its chief would not automatically be liable for an injury that occurred due to short stopping distance. If the maximum braking distance was 500 feet under certain road conditions, and the accident occurred in 400 feet, no liability would accrue since it would be technologically impossible for the officer to have had a better vehicle.

With the introduction of hydraulic brakes, however, the effective braking distances of automobiles was significantly reduced. If a police agency continued to use cars equipped with mechanical brakes, it would expose itself to liability if an officer or citizen were injured in a collision under circumstances similar to the previous example. If the available equipment would have permitted a stop without collision, the failure to equip could become the legal cause of the injury. Those responsible for the failure to equip safely might become liable for monetary damages.

The management of any organization that is involved in dangerous activities has a duty to upgrade the equipment whenever improved versions are widely available. The same duty applies to the upgrading of training and supervision. Failure to implement safety improvements would expose the agency and management to civil liability.

Citizens have a reasonable expectation that their officers are adequately trained in tactics and techniques, and can place criminals into custody with a minimum of danger to the community. It is a reasonable assumption that good tactics minimize the need for firearms use. It is also reasonable to assume that, when firearms must be used, officers will be sufficiently proficient to avoid injuring innocent citizens or themselves.

The arrestee also has an expectation that the police duty regarding his care will not be breached. Good tactics and techniques can ensure a minimum amount of injury to the violence-prone arrestee. If good tactics are used, the suspect may be deterred from an attempt to use a weapon; if good techniques are employed, he may be disarmed without being shot.

Police officers can also reasonably expect that the agency and management will not breach its duty of care to them. They can expect that their equipment, as well as their training and mandated tactics, will minimize their danger. The tactics and techniques that they are taught, and the way supervisors perform, should minimize their exposure to danger.

Civil liability

If no injury occurs, there will be no civil liability. Claims for money are made in cases where someone suffers injury, including damage to property, physical health, or future earnings. If there has been some injury, two questions are raised. The first is: "Was there a breach of a legal duty?" If no duty was breached, there will be no liability. If there was a breach, the second question to be asked is: "Was the breach of duty the proximate cause of the injury?"

In the police context, a major concern of the manager is

whether the injury to the citizen, the arrestee, or the police officer was foreseeable, due to the inadequate level of training or supervision.

This is always a fact question, requiring a jury to determine whether the level of training and supervision was adequate. A jury will determine whether the officer could have acted differently if the agency's training and supervision had been significantly different. The jury will also determine whether new, and available, standards of tactics and techniques would have prevented the injury.

The defense (the city and management) would argue that there was no breach of duty because the training and supervision were up to normal current standards. The defense might also argue that the injury was caused by the intervening action of the criminal.

The burden of convincing the jury that there was a management failure falls on the injured person, whether it be an innocent citizen, arrestee, or police officer.

Police tactics and techniques are technical issues, peculiar to the profession. Few attorneys have a good understanding of either the old or new principles regarding tactics and techniques. If the injuries are slight and the plaintiff's attorneys ill-prepared, the management and agency usually prevail. In cases where the injuries are great and the medical costs are large, a large monetary judgment is possible because of the injured party's incentive to research the areas of training and supervision.

A growing number of individuals across the country are now aware of the past failures regarding tactics and techniques. These experts are familiar with the newer standards and their value in minimizing injury. Injured officers (or spouses) will seek them out for technical advice and testimony at trials in the future. This will make it easier for the plaintiffs to show the wide gap between the high level of training and supervision that is possible . . . and that which existed at the time of the injury.

Police managers will not succeed by simply showing that *some* training occurred and that *some* supervision existed. If they cannot show that they discharged their duty responsibly, they will lose these suits. They must show that they provided training at the new levels of competency. They must prove that they were indeed in the world of hydraulic brakes rather than that of mechanical brakes. They must show that their departments were safe.

If they are unable to show that the danger was unforeseeable, then they will have large judgments awarded against them.

There are generally two levels of civil liability possible for these types of injuries. The lesser one is for negligent acts, the higher for reckless or intentional acts.

If a jury finds that there is liability and that the acts were performed negligently, the agency or management must pay a judgment sufficient to cover all the actual damages involved in the injury. Such a judgment can include medical charges, earnings, future wages, and an additional amount characterized as "pain and suffering." The greater the continuing pain on the part of the injured, the greater will be the monetary award for pain and suffering.

In many states, the agency is responsible for paying any judgment for the negligent acts of its employees. Often an insurance policy is in effect, and the insurance carrier pays the full judgment up to the limits of the policy.

In some states, there are limits to the amount that a governmental agency can pay. Whenever a judgment is greater than that amount, the plaintiff may seek the additional money through either a petition to the legislature or an additional claim against the employees for punitive damages.

When managers are found to have acted either recklessly or intentionally, most jurisdictions allow an additional award for punitive damages. This practice is designed to act as a deterrent to future reckless or intentional acts by the particular defendant, as well as others who might do the same thing.

The amount of the punitive damage award depends on two factors: the severity of the reckless/intentional act, and the financial ability of the defendant to pay. If the injury involves total disability, the award can be large. If the management personnel have large financial resources, a proportionately large amount may be awarded.

In jurisdictions where there is a low cap on the amount that an agency can pay, there is an incentive to the injured party to show that the individual managers were reckless or intentionally negligent in their training and supervision. In those cases, the smaller award against the agency can be augmented by the additional punitive awards.

Generally, in cases where the litigation is filed under the Federal Civil Rights Act, the plaintiff must show that the violation of the individual's civil rights was intentional. In these cases, the injured citizen, arrestee, or police officer would try to show that the management was aware of the low level of the training or supervision, and that the dangerous consequences were foreseeable. If he succeeds, the managers must pay the entire judgment.

In many cases, there is a strong economic incentive for an injured person to show that managers at various levels acted recklessly or intentionally. The injured person therefore tries to show that many people, from the chief on down, "knew or should have known" that the current procedures, tactics, and techniques were "unsafe." The more managers found to have been civilly liable, the more pockets can be tapped to pay the final judgment. If the jury finds that many were both legally responsible and "reckless," then many will pay.

Preventive action

The previously mentioned research has shown that injury to officers, as well as to innocent parties, can easily result if inadequate levels of tactics, techniques, and supervision prevail within an agency. A manager has a duty to his agency to minimize civil liability to it and its personnel. This can be achieved by establishing a continuing preventive action program.

Management should periodically review the current research in police tactics and techniques. The preferred responses to various tactical situations may vary, depending on the geography, criminal population, and technical environment.

It is important to remember that all agencies have a responsibility to develop guidelines that deal with the common tactical problems that their officers will face. The above considerations apply to weapons techniques and equipment.

"Hot pursuit" award in Arlington County, Virginia

Arlington County, Virginia, was ordered to pay $4.35 million to a bystander who lost both his legs as the result of a 1979 high-speed police chase after two bank robbers. Interest has increased the sum to more than $5 million.

The county appealed the judgment, rendered in January 1984, but that appeal was rejected without comment by the U.S. Supreme Court.

The case has been wrapped in controversy since the tragedy occurred on September 27, 1979. The incident began when Arlington County police officer Michael Kyle began a car chase of two suspected bank robbers. As the fleeing car crossed the border into Washington, D.C., the occupants allegedly fired shots at Kyle's car. The fleeing car then entered the busy downtown section of the city at a speed of 80 miles per hour, Kyle later reported. Witnesses said Kyle's car was not far behind, although Kyle maintained that he was too far away from the fleeing car to see it crash moments later. The crash caused pedestrian Alvin Biscoe to be pinned against a lamppost. Biscoe, who subsequently lost both legs, was a 50-year-old official with the National Science Foundation. He had been out for a lunch-time walk when the accident occurred.

Biscoe sued the driver of the fleeing car, who was later convicted of robbery, officer Kyle and Arlington County. In a 15-day trial in U.S. District Court in Washington in 1984, Biscoe's attorney, Joseph Koonz, noted that the Arlington County police department has a policy which expressly prohibits its officers from chasing suspects into Washington, D.C. or Maryland at speeds greater than 20 miles over the posted limit. The judgment against Arlington turned, at least in part, on the attorney's contention that Kyle was in violation of that policy at the time of the accident, the *Washington Post* reported.

The county argued that its sovereign immunity protected it from

Preventive action includes implementation of written guidelines for action in various tactical situations; adequate training including the new higher standards of tactics and techniques; provision of training time and equipment commitment needed to achieve the high standards; supervision to ensure that there is implementation of the guidelines, and supplementary training to maintain it; and continued monitoring of the competency levels of the personnel.

Written guidelines

The agency should determine the proper tactics and techniques for its service area. These should be written and distributed to all personnel. Officers must be aware of management's expectations regarding response to tactical situations. Guidelines can include the type of backup required in various cases and the methods of approaching arrest locations, such as automobiles on highways, apart-

---

having to pay Biscoe. Under Virginia law, jurisdictions are not liable for injuries that result from an employee's job performance. However, Judge Harold Greene ruled that sovereign immunity did not apply in the Biscoe case because the District of Columbia does not recognize that principle, the *Post* reported.

After the Supreme Court decision, Biscoe said at a press conference that he hoped the judgment would "send a message to police around the country. Police departments need to be more mindful of protecting the public first, and catching bank robbers second," he said. "I wonder if police departments have their heads on straight if they think it's more important to play cops and robbers than to protect the public."

The judgment against Arlington, said to be the largest "hot pursuit" award ever, will be paid by money set aside from county tax funds since 1982 in anticipation of the judgment, the *Post* reported. County Board Chairman John Milliken said the payment "will not have any current impact" on tax rates. The county was self-insured at the time of the accident.

The Arlington County police department has since revised its high speed pursuit policy by eliminating the section which restricts the speed at which vehicle pursuits can occur, Tom Bell of the Arlington police department told PRIMALETTER. "We changed the policy to give our officers more freedom," Bell said.

However, the police department recently received accreditation from the Commission on Accreditation for Law Enforcement Agencies. The commission requires a policy governing the pursuit of motor vehicles and the Arlington police department has an acceptable pursuit policy, according to James Cotter, executive director of the commission.

Source: February 1985 PRIMALETTER.

ments, single family dwellings, and business establishments. The officers should have written guidelines detailing the safest and most effective procedures, which should be updated as new research prompts improved tactics and techniques.

The use of guidelines makes it more likely that the safest procedures will be used. The written guidelines also make it easier to ensure uniformity of conduct and provide agency standards for evaluation of personnel. Officers who fall below the standards can be returned to duty after demonstrating competency in following the prescribed procedures. Those unable to meet the standards can be terminated or removed from operational assignments.

Training

Police work has become more sophisticated in recent years. The many analyses, including the federal task force reports, have

Police training

Sensitivity Training: teaches police officers to respond to the needs of people under extreme stress. Of special importance are potentially explosive domestic conflicts which often result in violence. The municipality must be certain to pay special attention to providing appropriate cultural sensitivity training to help officers in responding to the needs of constituent cultural groups.

Stress Management Courses: attempt to provide officers with techniques for dealing with the steadily increasing level of stress inherent in police work today. Stress management programs have the twofold benefit of reducing the possibility of police officers committing stress related errors on the job as well as lowering the possibility of officers experiencing stress associated health problems, such as heart attacks.

Civil Liability Courses: educate police officers as to the potential liabilities they may face in performing their duties. Training films in thhis area are widely available.

Weapons Training: include at least a semi-annual firearms qualification requirement as well as a "when-to-shoot" or combat course. Instruction should include proper cleaning, storage and safety of weapons while off duty. Also of importance is training in the use and effects of other weapons such as nightsticks, tear gas, and blackjacks.

Public Contact Programs: These programs seek to remove the psychological barrier between police departments and the public by providing direct contact between the two. One police department uses a "ride-along" program that puts volunteer citizen observers into patrol cars for a first-hand view of police work.

Highly screened and well-trained police officers are important factors in reducing civil liability exposures. Qualified police officers,

stressed the complexity of the police challenge. Recommendations have urged the development of skills in foreign languages, multicultural interrelationships, and the substantive and procedural laws.

While the intellectual demand placed on officers is increasing, the physical rigors of police work have not diminished. In fact, as the researchers show, they have increased. Police work is a physical profession and to survive and minimize injury to others, the police officer must have heightened physical, as well as intellectual, skills.

The officer must be trained in the intellectual concern for tactics. He must be able to analyze the initial problem and adjust his thinking to the changing conditions and actions of others at the scene. This training must utilize sophisticated teaching techniques in addition to the "talking head." The theory and substance of pertinent laws may initially be covered in a traditional manner, but such

---

however, are also in need of a clearly written policy concerning the use of deadly force. Once the policy is established it is important to strictly enforce it. A committee composed of high level officers should be established to review all applicable cases. A complete report should be filed and reviewed by a high ranking officer whenever an officer fires his/her weapon. Appropriate cases should be rreferred to the review board.

In addition, supervisors should be made responsible for identifying officers who are likely to use excessive force or other undesirable behavior. Officers found to be aggressive or violent unjustifiably should be subjected to departmental discipline or even dismissal.

Another important source of police civil liability suits emerges from bodily injury inflicted on bystanders during hot pursuit episodes. Police departments should construct a hot pursuit policy to emphasize the use of radios and roadblocks rather than dangerous high speed chases to apprehend fleeing suspects. Hot pursuit, if not prohibited, should be limited to use only for serious offenses.

Comment: There are many sources of exposure to police professional liability claims and an even greater number of approaches that attempt to control this exposure. Prudent police management dictates that a municipality do its utmost to safeguard its citizens from unnecessary injury inflicted by its law enforcement arm. By implementing effective risk control programs, municipalities can affirm their dedication to the protection of both constitutional rights of constituents as well as the municipal budget.

Source: *Governmental Risk Management Reports,* August 1981, a monthly periodical published by Risk Planning Group, division of Tillinghast, Nelson and Warren, Inc.

---

training must be supplemented by participation in scenarios where the officer must make decisions in lifelike settings. At the conclusion of each "problem," the training staff should reinforce the correct decisions and eliminate the dangerous ones. The student should be more competent after each session.

The physical aspects of police work must also be stressed and the motor skills developed within the subconscious mind. The officer must be able to use his hand, night stick, and gun with the necessary speed and accuracy. The decision to use the gun should be made intellectually, and the target selection must be made by the conscious mind. The subconscious mind must then control the muscles for quick action.

Tests have shown that motor skills are slow when the conscious mind must direct its attention to where the hand is in relationship to the gun butt or where the spare bullet pouch is located when reloading. These types of skills must be ingrained into the subconscious by constant drill.

In many cases, the criminal can fire a weapon in a second-and-a-half. To ensure the safety of the officer, his motor skill capacity must be adequate. When a conscious decision is made to fire in self-defense, the hand should grasp the gun, remove it from the holster, and fire it accurately in the right direction. This should occur rapidly. Failure could result in the death or injury of the officer or innocent third parties.

The conscious mind must be trained to analyze tactical problems and to act in an efficient, effective, and legal manner. The subconscious must be trained to direct the hands and weapons in an efficient manner at high speed when directed by the conscious mind.

It has also been shown that the time factor involved in attaining competence in both the conscious and subconscious area is much greater than was assumed in the past. Traditional training involved a minimum number of classroom hours and "range time." The testing, or "certification," had a low relationship to reality. It made no effort to deal with lifelike stressful scenarios.

If superficial amounts of training time and techniques were used, the officer will be at a significant disadvantage when he confronts danger. To ensure that the officer is capable of acting intelligently and effectively, more training time—both initially and on a continuing basis—will be required.

Supervision

After the training sessions have been completed, it is critical that the officers implement their training in day-to-day policing activities. One of the most important functions of first-line and upper-level supervision is to ensure that the correct procedures are implemented. Without continued supervision, the officers may fall back on old and dangerous procedures. Supervision should also constantly monitor officers' activities to determine when supplementary training is needed for individuals or for the whole agency.

A particularly important duty is to monitor the competence of the officers. Whenever an officer becomes physically, emotionally, or intellectually unable to perform to the standard, he should be removed from duty until the problem is solved.

An analogy would be the officer who becomes temporarily blinded. It is clear that if he is allowed to drive, liability would directly accrue to the supervisor if an injury occurred. Similarly, the capability and competency in the areas of tactics and techniques should be monitored so that individuals may be removed from dangerous areas until they can be rehabilitated or assigned to less dangerous posts.

Management success

If a police agency implements all of the above measures, it should minimize its exposure to civil liability. It will also maximize the safety of its officers and of the population. Appropriate management procedures maximize the efficiency of any organization and also minimize the possibility of monetary loss. Police managers always face new dangers, both physical and monetary. If they are constantly improving, they will face a safe and solvent future.

Summary

Recent research indicates that the current levels of job-related competency of most officers can lead to injury and death. New tactics and techniques can prevent a large number of these tragedies to officers, citizens, and arrestees. New training procedures can raise the level of competency of the officers to the new standards. Failure on the part of police managers to implement the new tactics and techniques can expose their agencies to civil liability. The same failure may also expose them to personal liability.

This exposure can be minimized by implementing guidelines that are appropriate to the policing problems of the particular jurisdiction. These guidelines must be coupled with effective and continuing training and supervision.

1. Ronal J. Adams, Thomas M. McTernan, Charles Remsberg, *Street Survival* (Evanston, Ill.: Calibre Press, 1980); Charles B. Moorman, Rich Wemmer, "Learning Points from Murders of California Law Enforcement Officers in 1978," *The Police Chief*, October 1979, p. 74. Eric Nielsen, Deen L. Eskridge, E. L. Willoughby, "Police Shooting Incidents," *The Police Chief*, July 1982, p. 44.

2. See "Focus, Weapons," *Law and Order*, September 1982, pp. 16–46, and recent issues of *Police Marksman* magazine. Organizations teaching new tactics and techniques include William Rogers, Rogers Holster Company, Jacksonville, Florida; Ray Chapman, Chapman Academy, Columbia, Missouri; Jeff Cooper, Gunsite Academy, Paulden, Arizona; Massad Ayoob, Lethal Force Institute, Concord, New Hampshire.

Police Liability Suits

Robert C. Vogt

In the handling of police professional liability cases there are two axioms. One, as long as police can be sued and law enforcement actions take place, lawsuits will take place. You cannot stop all the lawsuits but you can control them. Two, *document! document! document!* If you do not document an action, an order, or an event, it did not take place in the eyes of the judicial system.

Liability for law enforcement suits can originate from two distinct sources. One, your own negligent actions and two, the negligent actions of others. The negligent actions of others, giving rise to liability for supervisors and superiors is known as vicarious liability. Vicarious liability is the legal doctrine whereby the negligent acts of subordinates are transferred to their superiors.

Liability from direct action can fall into several broad categories; including but not limited to:

1. Abuse of or excessive use of force
2. Illegal search and seizure
3. Coercion to obtain confessions
4. Assault and battery (nearly all arrests can be alleged to have involved assault and battery)
5. Cruel and unusual treatment of prisoners.

Any of the above direct actions can be direct allegations made in a suit or can lead or provide the basis for allegations of constitutional rights violations.

Reprinted with permission from "Sources of Police Professional Liability Suits, Preventive Measures and Defense Techniques," in the January 1984 issue of *Governmental Liability Reporter*, published by Markel Service, Inc.

The treatment of prisoners or allegations involving jail conditions can involve a wide variety of complaints. Some of the most common would include (1) lack of or improper medical care, (2) unsanitary conditions, (3) placing of inmates in cells with other inmates with known violent propensities, (4) overlooking continuing physical abuse or sexual activities of prisoners, (5) allowing a "kangaroo court' by inmates, (6) cruel and unusual punishment and (7) overcrowding.

The indirect or vicarious liability, while not being legally defined, was first introduced for law enforcement liability in a 1979 ruling, *McClelland* v. *Facteau,* which held that administrators can be held liable personally for the actions of subordinates. There are, fundamentally, seven actions of administrators which can give rise to vicarious liability. These are affectionately referred to as "the seven deadly sins": (1) *negligent hiring*—there is a duty to "weed out" the obviously unfit; (2) *failure to direct*—a written policies and procedures manual is a must; (3) *failure to train*—proper instruction in the use of firearms, tear gas, administration of medical care, and traffic control is essential; (4) *negligent supervision*—all administrators have a duty to know what subordinates are doing; either they know or they should have known; (5) *negligent assignment*—assigning the wrong man for a particular job can give rise to vicarious liability; (6) *negligent retention*—once a problem area is known the administrator must act to eliminate the problem; (7) *negligent entrustment*—the issuance of a gun, night stick or vehicle to an employee which is subsequently used in an off-duty action, in moonlighting employment, or in actions outside the scope of his duties, can result in vicarious liability.

Preventive measures

There are many actions and procedures that can be taken by the administrator which can prevent a suit from being filed or mitigate the circumstances surrounding a particular law enforcement action, thereby strengthening a defense of a particular suit.

1. *Document! Document! Document!* Paperwork is often seen as a necessary evil by administrators and normally as a hindrance to their job by the line officer. However, every action, well documented can only help to further the defense of a suit.
2. *Procedures manual.* Most of the seven deadly sins and several other sources of liability can be controlled by a well written procedures manual that is both (1) complete and (2) enforced.
3. *Updating/revision of procedures manual.* As various court decisions are handed down, the rules are changed. A revision of procedures on an established, periodic basis must be established.

4. *Training and testing.* This is again an ongoing process. Training and testing only new recruits is a piecemeal approach.
5. *Retroactive application of testing and training.* A new test or requirement must be applied to all personnel regardless of seniority. As an example, despite a new requirement for psychological testing, a veteran officer was not required to take the psychological testing, and was found, after an "unfortunate" event, to be unacceptable and unfit for his position from a psychological standpoint. Needless to say, a lawsuit based on vicarious liability was filed, and since no retroactive testing was enforced, it is very difficult to defend such a suit.
6. *Creation of a review/complaint committee.* Having an adequate means of redress, before a board comprised of lay people and those without a vested interest, can provide a forum for the venting of frustrations and resolve a great percentage of *potential* suits. Many suits are filed simply out of frustration and anger. Providing an alternative means of venting this anger is much more cost effective than defending a liability suit, not to mention the benefits in public relations.
7. *Creation of a peer counseling program.* It is essential to prevent "burnout" and the proliferation of "attitude" problems by the use of encounter groups and rap sessions. Bringing the "choir boys" syndrome out of the bars and parks and into a controlled environment with a trained staff can prevent a host of problems.

Legal defense techniques

There are several defense techniques which are either unknown or unused by many defense attorneys.

Before considering these techniques, ask yourself if the attorney you have retained is a plaintiff's attorney or a defense attorney? How can a plaintiff's attorney be expected to be competent on the defense side of the bench? Also, is the attorney experienced in municipal defense? Can you afford to let the attorney "go to school" on your case? Can a contract specialist or an auto liability specialist be expected to properly handle your law enforcement liability defense?

Three basic techniques have been effectively pursued. These are (1) a motion for summary judgment, (2) a request for admission of no liability and (3) institution of a countersuit.

Motion for summary judgment A motion for summary judgment is a petition to the court for an immediate dismissal of a case based on a lack of genuine issue or material fact presented in the particulars of the complaint before the court. This motion may be made at almost any point in the legal proceedings when it is best or most advantageous to the particular defense strategy. This technique is seen as a "no lose" situation. Even if the motion is denied, the plaintiff's attorney is forced to "show his cards" to demonstrate that his complaint has merit. Affidavits, supporting documents, names of potential witnesses or experts all must be revealed by the plaintiff's attorney. This valuable information would obviously be advantageous to the defense.

Request for admission of no liability A request for admission of no liability is made of the plaintiff's attorney and filed with the court. It simply asks the plaintiff to admit that there is no factual basis to support the claim relating to all allegations and defendants or to particular issues and defendants. This is particularly effective when the "shotgun" approach has been taken by the plaintiff, whereby the plaintiff names all possible individuals as defendants and alleges a wide variety of complaints, hoping to have one or a few complaints or defendants upheld at trial. The plaintiff's attorney cannot claim a lack of knowledge or information in his response. He has but three choices. He may (1) admit the request, (2) ignore the request, which will have the same effect, or (3) deny the request.

If the request is denied, and the *defendant* is successful in his defense, he may be entitled to reasonable attorney's fees! This is a very effective way to have the suit pared to only those issues that are real and material, as the plaintiff will rarely risk paying the defendant's attorney's fees for a frivolous and meritless issue.

Countersuits Countersuits are often overlooked but are a very effective means to stop the proliferation of nuisance suits. Are an increasing number of suits found from a particular segment of the population or from one or two attorneys who specialize in this area? Just who is guilty of harassment or excessive use of (judicial) force. When insurance companies "buy off" one or two claims for a "modest" settlement, to escape the high cost of defense, the world will beat a path to your door. The filing of a countersuit will force the plaintiffs and their attorneys to "think twice" about frivolous and meritless suits.

Obviously, we have not exhausted the possibilities for sources of police professional liability suits nor have we covered all possible preventive or defense techniques. However, by reviewing your department in light of the information provided, a good first step in controlling your liability exposure would have been taken.

Understanding the Full Pollution Exclusion

David Dybdahl

Environmental impairment has become a very "hot" political and social issue. As the movement toward cleaning the environment and compensating victims gathers momentum, many risk managers are finding insurance coverage for this exposure difficult to find. This article will offer an analysis of how this situation has come about and how the public risk manager can best handle pollution exposures given current market restrictions.

"Let the polluter pay"

Most federal and state laws that relate to cleaning the environment were formulated on the basis of "let the polluter pay." However, the use of this concept frequently means that the polluter's *insurer* pays, and with the courts awarding millions of dollars to victims of environmental contamination, insurance companies are finding that they are faced with claims they did not intend to cover. The insurance industry's response to this situation is very predictable. Currently, many insurance carriers are including a full pollution exclusion (excluding both sudden and accidental, and non-sudden or gradual pollution) on all comprehensive general liability (CGL) and umbrella contracts issued to public entities.

This exclusion is of concern to public risk managers because most public entities do face environmental impairment liability loss exposures. For example, almost all public entities are involved in waste disposal. Even if an entity is not currently involved in waste disposal, environmental liabilities are retroactive and are not cov-

Reprinted with permission from the March 1985 issue of PRIMALETTER, published by the Public Risk and Insurance Management Association, Washington, D.C.

ered by a statute of limitations. Further, most entities have also been involved with the generation and transportation of waste, and are liable for exposures arising out of these activities as well. Also, most public entities store fuels underground, and northern entities maintain storage facilities for road salt; both represent possible pollution exposures. Hospitals and universities also represent pollution exposures.

To determine the extent of pollution coverage needed, the risk manager should take inventory of possible pollution exposures. This can be done through surveys and by conducting risk assessments of those facilities that pose a substantial risk.

A major exposure: landfills

In a report to Congress dated December 12, 1984, the U.S. Environmental Protection Agency (EPA) estimated that 12,000 to 18,000 municipal landfills and dumps are currently operating in the United States; nearly twice that number may be closed or abandoned. Many of these facilities routinely accepted hazardous wastes before the practice was outlawed by the Resource Conservation and Recovery Act (RCRA) of 1976. Some sites still accept hazardous wastes from small-quantity generators and households.

Further, many closed and/or abandoned dump sites also represent a serious environmental risk. To deal with this problem, the Comprehensive Environmental Response Compensation and Liability Act (CERCLA) was passed in 1980. This law authorized the creation of a "Superfund" to clean up old or abandoned hazardous waste sites and provided funds for emergency response to pollution incidents. To fund the bill, Congress appropriated $1.6 billion.

To implement the Superfund, the EPA first identified as many old or abandoned sites as possible, and then ranked the sites according to various parameters designed to determine the possibility of immediate and/or severe environmental degradation. Nearly 22,000 sites were identified, and 786 of them are listed as "priority" sites for clean-up. One of every five such sites is either owned by a municipality or contains municipal wastes.

Following the concept that polluters should pay for cleanup, the Superfund is designed to pay for only a fraction of the cost of clean-up/compensation at each site. The law requires that the federal government seek to recover cleanup costs from responsible parties, including generators and transporters of the waste, and past, present and future owners of the site. The Justice Department is authorized to prosecute for collection of cleanup costs under legal theories of strict, joint and several liability.

If current trends continue, the insurance industry may be saddled with the bulk of all environmental impairment, restoration and victim compensation claims. It is a financial burden that the insurance industry cannot absorb. In 1984, the property and casualty industry lost $6 billion in "paid in capital" and surplus. It was one of the worst years in the history of the industry. The total equity for the insurance industry is now $60 billion, after 1984 losses. The predicted price tag for providing cleanup and victim compensation for all of the Superfund sites alone ranges from $12 billion to $100 billion. If forced to pay claims of that magnitude, many individual insurance companies with large books of general liability insurance will be in financial peril. The insurance industry's response to this situation is the full pollution exclusion.

Pollution exclusions: a history

The International Services Office (ISO) introduced a non-sudden pollution exclusion in 1973 that limited coverage under CGL, umbrella, and errors and omissions policies to sudden and accidental pollution. However, in many cases involving non-sudden pollution, such as landfill contamination, the courts have held that the pollution exclusion does not apply. These court interpretations threaten to leave the insurance industry in dire straits.

Insurance companies have responded to this situation by limiting their exposure. The ISO has developed two options for limiting environmental exposures on a CGL policy. One is to issue a claims-made policy form; the other, more common, option is the full pollution exclusion, designed to eliminate even sudden and accidental coverage from the CGL form. Rates are being developed for the buy-back of sudden and accidental pollution coverage, although many carriers are not planning to make this extension of coverage available. Lloyd's of London has also proposed a new "first claims-made" liability form that would substantially reduce the exposure period on environmental claims.

Finding pollution coverage

The current position of the insurance industry on environmental impairment liability will probably frustrate many public risk managers seeking to renew coverage this year. To fill the gap in insurance coverage, a risk manager has basically two options: buying back the sudden and accidental pollution coverage on the CGL and umbrella policies; or purchasing EIL coverage.

As previously mentioned, most carriers are not providing the buy-back option at this time. Also, risk managers should recognize that sudden and accidental coverage is only a partial risk transfer for environmental losses. The most expensive environmental losses occur over time, and these non-sudden losses would still be excluded under the non-sudden pollution exclusion on the CGL policy.

The second option is to purchase EIL coverage. EIL policies are designed specifically to cover bodily injury and property damage arising from non-sudden environmental impairment. These policies can be endorsed to include sudden and accidental coverage. The risk manager faced with the sudden and accidental pollution exclusion on his CGL policy can fill that gap in coverage by including sudden and accidental pollution coverage on an EIL policy. However, this option, like the EIL policy itself, may not be readily available.

The market for EIL coverage has never been very large. With the hardening of the insurance market place, the number of carriers willing to write this coverage has shrunk dramatically. Those remaining are also offering much smaller limits than in previous years. Basically, for monoline EIL coverage, the only two markets left in the U.S. are AIG and Swett and Crawford. The Pollution Liability Insurance Association, a reinsurance pool of 40 insurance companies, is still a viable market for EIL coverage., but it does not offer this coverage on a monoline basis. Also, some larger carriers offer EIL insurance to their larger customers who have incidental environmental liability exposures. The risk manager should ask his broker or agent about available options.

Conclusion

Risk managers seeking to insure environmental losses will face a very restrictive market. Most carriers that provide sudden and accidental pollution coverage in the past will seek to exclude it on renewal. The remaining monoline EIL carriers are able to be very choosy about which risks they underwrite. In order to overcome the hard market, a risk manager must be able to show that his organization has been actively involved in risk identification and loss prevention and control.

PART 4

Risk Control in the Workplace

Management and the Safety Function

Don LeMond

Is safety really first?

Years ago it was quite fashionable to quote the slogan "Safety First." Let us put that old slogan to rest by emphasizing what top management has always known. Safety is not and cannot be first. It is profits, mission, product, service and the strength and growth of the organization that are first. Safety is important because it can either support or damage these things; it is not something separate, a function by itself. Safety is concerned with all the functions of an organization and should be fully integrated into those functions, not merely imposed as an afterthought.

Safety as a management resource

A government is a system composed of many subsystems. There are financial systems, personnel systems, production systems, maintenance systems, etc. Any accident, injury, unsafe act, workplace health problem or unsafe condition indicates a failure in the system. Safety personnel act as system evaluators, advising management on how functional parts of the system should operate with regard to safety and health. Safety thus becomes a resource to get the job done, not just a burden that hampers the system.

For example, consider a ladder in a stockroom which breaks when a clerk climbs to a high storage bin. We might typically find that the ladder had not been properly and regularly inspected (a lower management error). Asking why this happened, we might

---

Reprinted with permission from the February 1984 issue of PRIMALETTER, published by the Public Risk and Insurance Management Association, Washington, D.C.

find that a procedure for regular inspection of ladders had not been established (a management failure); that the regulations regarding inspection were not known (a management failure); that such ladders were of an inferior quality and should not have been purchased in the first place (a staff failure); and that funds to purchase proper equipment were not made available (staff and management failures). A closer review of the overall operation might show that these management and staff failures were also causing similar problems throughout the organization, including costly delays and difficulties, worker unrest, and labor organization concern over the use of unsafe equipment.

Baltimore promotes safety

Following is a description of the program that won PRIMA's safety in the workplace award in 1984.

PRIMA's panel of judges was impressed. For only $20,000, Baltimore's Office of Occupational Medicine and Safety had launched an innovative, multifaceted safety awareness campaign for the city's 35,000 employees. That program, launched on July 1, 1980, has helped to reduce accidents by 16%, workers compensation claims by 13%, and the cost of those claims by 17%, according to David Rule, deputy director of the safety office.

The safety awareness campaign "is aimed at the individual employee," Rule said. "This employee is given proper recognition and respect through our entire program. In essence, city management says to the employee: 'We recognize your problems. We respect you enough to do whatever is required to provide you with a safe and healthful work environment.'"

The program's objectives follow those listed in the National Safety Council Accident Prevention Manual:

1. Help develop safe work habits and safe attitudes
2. Focus attention on specific causes of accidents
3. Supplement safety training
4. Give the employee a chance to participate in accident prevention activities
5. Provide a channel of communication between workers and management
6. Improve employee, and public, relations.

Safety: "a mark of skill"

The safety awareness campaign itself was launched with a safety slogan contest, open to all city employees. The winning slogan was "Work Safely, Safety Works"; the winner received a one-year family membership to Baltimore's new national aquarium. Mayor William Schaefer presented awards to the winner and 24 runners-up at an

From a simple broken rung we thus detect several cause factors and many examples of poor management and staff work. Once such conditions are recognized and corrected, the entire operation will improve.

Safety as a management function

There is little difference between the safety function and any other organizational function. As with any other function, management should direct the safety effort by setting realistic goals, and by planning, organizing and establishing controls for the program. While management may assign responsibility and authority for safety to

---

official ceremony which received local press coverage. The slogan was then promoted on bumper stickers, agency correspondence and posters.

Another key element of the safety awareness program is the safety bulletin board. Each of the city's 900 permanent work sites is required to have such a bulletin board posted where all employees can view it at least once per work shift. The safety office distributes these items for posting on the bulletin boards: a Maryland Occupational Safety and Health poster, off-the-job safety posters, the Baltimore safety office newsletter, safety bulletins and departmental and work site news bulletins and notices. Also included are National Safety Council posters which target a particular problem, hazard or area for intense analysis and improvement. On the back of these posters, the safety office types information which site supervisors and managers can use in talking to their employees about the targeted problem.

Rule explained that the off-the-job accident posters are posted to demonstrate the city's "holistic concern for them [the workers] as citizens and not just as employees. We recognize that off-the-job accidents can directly affect on-the-job productivity."

Rule's office also publishes two newsletters: a safety newsletter, distributed quarterly to all work sites and the newsletter of its Safety Officers Association, which is a group of safety officers and representatives from all city agencies. "As a group, we try to help one another with mutual problems, assisting each other through discussion and direct implementation of solutions we have found at other agencies." The office also publishes safety bulletins, as needed.

To enforce and promote the mandatory regulation that each work site have a safety bulletin board, the safety office awards a blue ribbon to each site whose bulletin board has all the proper and updated documents. "While it is a massive task to visit almost 900 permanent city work sites, this does allow the safety officers to get out into the field and view the work sites first-hand. From these visits, other appropriate safety tasks such as inspections or investigations might result," Rule said.

Safety information is not only displayed on the bulletin boards; posters often appear throughout the work sites. "This fosters the atti-

the line managers, and hold them accountable for the results, management must assume the overall accountability and responsibility.

Line and staff managers, of course, can and should be held accountable for those safety functions which they can control. To use the previous illustration, we cannot hold the purchasing department responsible for the storeroom clerk's actions in climbing the defective ladder. However, the purchasing department can be held responsible for buying an inferior and possibly unapproved product—if it had been provided with the resources and direction necessary for purchasing the proper equipment. Perhaps we cannot hold

---

tude among employees that accidents are mistakes and that not having accidents is a mark of skill," Rule said.

The bulletin boards are used to promote another facet of the safety awareness program—a safety suggestion campaign. Employees recognizing real or potential problems or possible improvements to their work or city environment are encouraged to contact the safety office. "However, we do require that our employees think through the problem and submit a solution with their suggestion," Rule said. "Obviously, any immediate work hazard should be corrected quickly by the unit supervisor. However, some are not and this is one way our central safety office is made aware of these hazards out in the field." Each year, a grand prize winner and an unspecified number of runners-up are chosen from those submitting suggestions during the year. The grand prize winner receives five days of paid leave; the runners-up each receive one day of paid leave. Once again, prizes are awarded by Mayor Schaefer in an official ceremony. "More importantly," Rule notes, "we try to implement all of the safety suggestions submitted to this office."

Safety awareness month

In 1983, Mayor Schaefer designated October as Safety Awareness Month. During that month, a Safety-at-the-Work-Site Week and a safety display contest were held.

The Safety-at-the-Work-Site Week was a project of the city's Joint Labor Management Safety Committee, a coalition of employee organizations and city management personnel formed to promote and support safety in Baltimore. The first day of the special week was launched with a mayoral proclamation and ceremony, followed by lunch time activities at a public plaza which all city employees were invited to attend. Events included demonstrations by various agencies, safety exhibits, entertainment, and distribution of safety literature, prizes and gifts.

During the week that followed, all work units conducted safety activities, including: talks, demonstrations, presentations, films, training, and inspections and investigations concerned with the specific problems of that work unit.

---

the safety office personnel responsible for an accident in the storeroom over which they have no direct control, but we can hold them responsible and accountable if inadequate purchasing guidance exists. Likewise, it is their responsibility to conduct equipment inspections and advise management on the need for certain guidelines and procedures.

Evaluating the safety function

Evaluation of a governmental organization's involvement in safety can begin with the following questions:

To promote the safety week, a safety display contest was also held. Each work unit was eligible to submit a display which focused on that site's particular hazards. A plaque and a certificate of congratulations from the mayor were awarded to winners in six categories: Most original; most effective; most eye-catching; most interesting; most entertaining; and most colorful.

The safety office has also established a Joint Labor Management Employee Assistance Committee. "While this committee is aimed at addressing certain individual problems with our employees, which may include alcohol and drugs, we found that we cannot separate their mission from our total safety program. Thus, we join with this committee to promote safety through the treatment of known employee problems," Rule said.

At the city's central clinic for employees, the safety office provides safety counseling, which includes "a review of that accident and may lead to further investigation or inspection of the work site." "We also try to give that employee an understanding of what occurred and how it might be prevented in the future," Rule said.

Rule noted that the safety office regularly uses National Safety Council items and gifts. "Two very popular items with city employees include the distribution of keychains and the small personal first-aid kits. For some reason the employees are very gratified to receive them and we hope they use them to further the good impression of safety in their job and life," Rule said.

In the future, Rule in planning to raise money for a safety awareness fund which would be used to promote safety and present awards to those employees and units who display particular achievements in safety. He would also like to establish a Mayor's Safety Award, which would be given to the agency or work unit displaying the best safety performance for a given time period. His safety office is currently working on an in-house computer information system which would provide the quantitative data to "fairly and equitably choose a winner." The award would be a trophy that would be passed from one winning unit to the next. The trophy would be presented by the mayor at a cabinet meeting, Rule said.

Source: August 1984 PRIMALETTER.

1. Is there a formal safety policy? What is it and who knows it?
2. How is safety built into the organization?
3. Where is the safety function located in the organization? To whom is the function responsible?
4. What are the line and staff relationships on safety and health?
5. Where is the health function within the organization? To whom is the function responsible?
6. How are line safety and health responsibilities defined?
7. How does management hold line and staff accountable for safety and health?
8. How are senior management or senior administrators held accountable and rated in terms of safety and health?
9. How is staff measured in safety and health performances?
10. How are supervisors measured in safety and health performance?

These questions require more than simple answers, so be prepared for an in-depth look at the organization.

Avoidance of loss

Peter Drucker, author of several books about management, has said that "it is the first duty of business to survive. The guiding principle is not the maximization of profits, *but the avoidance of loss.*"

This "avoidance of loss" characterizes the safety function very well. Operating errors produce accidents, injuries and economic losses. These operating errors and unplanned events occur mostly when human and physical resources are badly handled. Locating operational errors is a good management technique for loss avoidance as well as a sound safety management approach.

A manager should see unwanted or unplanned events in terms of: skill deficiencies; poor supervision; fiscal mismanagement and unwise decision making.

Unwanted events, in turn, translate directly into: excessive maintenance; cost overruns; slippage; downtime; and wastage. These easily recognized management terms fully apply to occupational safety and health functions.

The loss control concept

The loss control concept, as some refer to safety and health management, also reflects this view. The loss control concept holds that safety and health management should " . . . locate and define operational errors involving incomplete decision-making, faulty judgment, administrative miscalculations, and plain honest-to-goodness bad management and individual practices leading to incidents which downgrade the system; and provide sound advice to management as to how such mistakes can be avoided."

The circle is complete. Safety management operates exactly the same way as any other management function. Its aims and goals are the same as management's overall objectives.

The supervisor

The supervisor generally has little time to be a creative manager. His duties are usually prescribed, and are so demanding that he must concentrate primarily on those responsibilities emphasized by upper management. He is the last in a line of managers and may often be the "fall" guy who, while not given the resources to do his job properly, is still held responsible for worker safety and health. Finally, while he may be the closest manager to the actual work tasks being carried out, he may have the least say over the safety and health aspects of those tasks.

Attaining safety objectives

The ideal safety program should have the same objectives that underlie any other management function. Let us look at what authors Peter Drucker and Warren Bennis have said about the "multiple objectives of business" and discuss some of the safety implications:

1. *Profitability.* This business objective, readily understood by government managers, refers to management's desire to maximize profits (or avoid losses). Reducing services, personnel and equipment costs are part of making operations more profitable. Accidents and injuries cost money, thus reducing "profits." Safety, therefore has an impact on profitability.
2. *Productivity.* This is directly influenced by time-consuming accidents which shut down a production line, delay deliveries, incapacitate skilled operators, destroy essential equipment, etc. Less easily measured but just as detrimental to production is the loss of efficiency and morale which occurs after a serious accident or incident.
3. *Amount of resources.* Whenever accidental losses occur, the overall amount of resources are depleted. Money that could be used for more profitable pursuits may have to be diverted to solve needless safety and health losses.
4. *Service.* When safety and health problems occur, the ability to give quality service is reduced. Unsafe equipment, moreover, can result in enormous service costs if repair or replacement is necessary.
5. *Innovation.* The development of new services is often essential. The proliferation of new standards and regulations and the need to incorporate costly safety and health considerations radically affect innovation from initial concept through design and implementation.

6. *Social contribution.* This is synonymous with public responsibility. Consider the cost to society (and in turn, to government) of rehabilitating an injured worker, supporting his family, and the overall social cost of losing a skilled, productive member of society.
7. *Identification.* This involves a management and staff commitment to the same organization objectives. Safety and health issues can seriously divide management and staff unless management and staff *both* understand that safety is directly tied to the prime objectives of the organization.
8. *Social influence.* Effective safety and health performance should become an expectation. To achieve this expectation, responsibility and accountability must be placed throughout the organization.
9. *Collaboration.* Safety and health issues may involve conflicts or problems between staff and management. Effective management will focus on safety and health as a common goal which needs cooperation at all levels.
10. *Adaptation.* Every organization must continually meet changing environmental and technological requirements and regulations. Management must also recognize that it is facing a new climate of public awareness about safety and health.
11. *Integration.* Overlapping objectives and responsibilities help make a smooth operation. Integration may be especially crucial for safety and health functions, which cannot be confined to a single department.

Management's responsibility for safety

In times when economy of operation is necessary, management seeks to reduce costs by streamlining operations, cutting back on equipment purchases, reducing stockpiles, tightening up on maintenance, increasing efficiency of production and cutting down on overhead personnel. Safety and health activities are frequently among those considered superfluous. The manager who sees safety and health as a marginal activity is overlooking its potential for great monetary savings and productive improvement without costly expenditures, and cutbacks on operations, personnel or services.

This systematic way to achieve savings stems from the simple assumption that *all accidents and hazards are indications of management failures.* Radical as this assumption may seem, the approach is one that has been widely used in industry and can be applied to all types of organizations. These same management failures can cause many production and service losses, as well. Investigations have shown that these failures often go on for years, causing large, cumulative losses without anyone being aware of them.

In investigating an accident, one can always find some degree of management involvement or activity that might have prevented the event in some way. Applying this theory, the investigation of each hazard, accident, and injury is directed toward identifying the underlying management problem. Management here refers to all levels of management above the first-line supervisor and includes all staff and support functions such as administrative, supply, maintenance, security and safety personnel. It excludes the immediate supervisor because the key to prevention and correction lies above the supervisor. This distinction is not meant to lessen the supervisor's role, but rather to place the power of correction where it realistically belongs.

Applying the system

In investigating each event a single question must be applied at every turn: "Where did management fail?" Seek to find what management did or did not do that permitted the event or situation to occur. In some cases the management failures will be obvious. In others they will be remote and indistinct, but they will always be present. This technique need not be confined to accidents or injuries; it is just as appropriate to use the system in any unusual event which indicates that the organization is not performing as it should.

There is no reason to feel defensive about a system that deliberately seeks out management's failures or, more precisely, failures in the structure and systems. Ultimately, it will benefit management's real interests. Prompt attention to management's inefficiencies will also indicate management's concern for, and interest in, personnel. Such a system will earn appreciation and boost employee morale.

Managing the Greatest Risk Cost: Health Care

For the first time in a decade it appears that inflation may be subsiding. Recent indicators are encouraging. However, the momentum of spiraling health care cost increases continues unabated. In fact, the increase in health care costs is a national problem—with crisis implications, Since 1967, medical costs have more than tripled, with hospital rates quintupling. Total health care expenditures in this country have soared to over 10% of our gross national product compared to approximately 5% less than 30 years ago. The U.S. is now spending more than twice as much for health care as defense (debate of the latter is more politically palatable). The health care industry has become the nation's third largest employer after civil service and retailing. Interestingly, next to Germany, as a percentage of gross national product (GNP), our expenditures for health care are the second highest in the world. Even Britain, with its grandiose health care program, spends approximately half as much as the U.S. as a percentage of GNP. The recent increases of 15 to 20% a year in this sector of the economy cannot continue indefinitely. Yet the gradual aging of our population, combined with rapidly advancing medical technology, make any change in past patterns very remote. Something has got to give!

There are a multitude of reasons why health care costs are out of control. A shortage of nurses, excessive in-hospital treatment, and the third-party system of payment (combined with the tax-deductibility status of health care) all contribute to the problem.

Reprinted from the August 1983 issue of *Governmental Risk Management Reports*, a monthly periodical published by Risk Planning Group, division of Tillinghast, Nelson and Warren, Inc.

The central issue compounding inefficiencies is that the physician makes most of the major decisions affecting the quality and extent of treatment. Unfortunately, there is little incentive for him/her to make decisions on the basis of expense.

Is there any way to alter the countervailing health care trend? Certainly, as with any problem, there are solutions available. One of the unanswered questions is whether our populace is willing to accept changes in delivery procedures that may be necessary to produce more cost-conscious medical treatment. National trends will not be altered easily.

On an individual basis, a municipality can control the cost of its health care program. One ground rule, however, is that the plan must be structured so there is *control* over the plan design, claims processing and the development of management information for monitoring the program. This will generally involve an aggressively funded contract with an administrator/carrier adept at claims processing and management information reporting.

We believe the reason to take charge of the administration of a health program is to be able to exert more control over the delivery of this benefit. Unless a plan sponsor so structures the administrative apparatus as to be directly responsible for the claims experience, there is little incentive to implement sound cost-containment principles, which will result in the large, long-range dollar savings in any health care plan.

Of course, there will be some employers where, because of size or experience, it is impractical to pursue any approach other than enrollment in a pooled or fully insured situation.

There has been too much emphasis in the past on the pros and cons of the "mechanical" element of self-insurance, and not nearly enough on the real rationale for taking control of the administration of this particular benefit area. Only by taking the initiative to get directly involved in an aggressively funded program, where there is responsibility for claims experience, will the needed impetus be present to incorporate cost-containment principles that affect the consumption of medical services.

Since there is a big difference in the quality of claims administrators, the selection process in choosing the right firm is crucial to the success in containing health care costs. Once the proper funding and administrative apparatus is in place, cost-containment principles applicable to a municipality's employees can be explored and implemented on a gradual basis.

Examples of cost-containment techniques might include the following:

1. Based on a review of claims over the past two years, determine the most frequent minor surgical operations performed. Offer the incentive of 100% coverage with no deductible if

such surgery is performed on an out-patient basis. Implement greater than usual deductibles and coinsurance percentages if the same surgery is performed in-hospital. This will encourage employees to ask physicians and surgeons if scheduled surgery can be done on a lower-cost out-patient basis.

2. Encourage second surgical opinions at no charge. If major surgery is involved, make second surgical opinions mandatory. If they are not obtained, institute a higher-than-normal deductible and coinsurance percentage as a penalty.
3. Cover doctor office visits at 100% for most minor procedures, e.g., flu shots, children's accidents, etc. and implement higher than normal deductibles and coinsurance percentages for treatment at emergency centers vs. a doctor's office.
4. Offer maternity patients the incentive of household help for one week for cooking, cleaning and child care if they leave the hospital the second or third day after delivery.
5. Provide 100% coverage for hospice treatment. Doctors and nurses who work in these institutions are generally more dedicated to the treatment of the terminally ill patients than those in general hospitals. The thrust of hospice care is to alleviate physical pain and emotional suffering, and can be a more pleasant and realistic alternative for terminally ill patients. The cost is considerably less (approximately ⅓) than in-hospital care.

In addition to the above, subtle preventive medicine and "*stay well*" tactics can be added to the program. Examples include the payment of fees for attendance at smoke-ending treatment centers, consultations concerning alcohol and drug abuse, and biennial hypertension screening for all employees over 40 years of age.

Once source of economical, efficient health care that continues to be overlooked and short-changed by many municipalities is HMOs. Many of the cost-containment principles being advocated today in the more progressive group plans originated with HMOs, where the efficient delivery of medical benefits is vital to the ongoing success of the organization. It is being proven that many HMOs can operate profitably; they provide ongoing documentation that cost-containment procedures work if administered effectively.

A hybrid approach to medical protection which lies between the unlimited options available to employees under the standard group plan, and the more rigid structure of an HMO are the "preferred provider networks" springing up around the country. These arrangements take advantage of a prescreened list of doctors and hospitals that offer discounts to plan sponsors in return for a "free referral service" sponsored by the employer. Coverage might be provided at 100% reimbursement if employees use the preferred providers, thus giving incentives to use this prescreened group. Both of these more efficient methodologies of delivering health care to employees warrant serious investigation by municipal employers.

Another area to consider is cost sharing with employees. This can take the form of higher deductibles, higher coinsurance percentages, and employee contributions. For instance, $300 or $500 deductibles and 70% coinsurance provisions discourage nuisance claims and encourage employees to seek out the most efficient forms of treatment. This strategy can be combined with a "bonus" program, whereby favorable plan experience is passed back to employees at year-end in the form of a bonus, ranging from $100 to $500. Some employers have instituted programs where employees who file no claims have a flat amount (e.g., $250) "banked" for them on an annual basis. The objective is to encourage and reward employee cooperation in using health care coverage efficiently. Note that some employers have not found contributory plans cost-effective, as there is the normal human tendency for employees to use the plan, no matter what, since they "are paying for it anyway." Conversely, high deductible programs shift more of the cost onto those using the plan.

In the administrative area a risk manager can have all health claims over a predetermined amount, say $20,000, audited by an independent third-party specialist. The audit can ascertain whether or not the current administrator is doing an effective and competent job of processing claims (are they only paying for services rendered, and necessary, etc.?).

Governmental entities don't have to lose out to rising health care costs. Control requires a combination of management time, retaining the proper expertise to assist in re-designing a program, and the services of a competent outside administrator to assist with effective claims management. Unless municipalities act quickly on their own, the federal government may eventually legislate its own "solutions." Proposed legislation limiting the value of health benefits that can be received tax-free by employees is currently being considered in Congress as one option to "cap" these costs.

One of the obstacles to implementing a more efficient medical program is unions. We have found they can be particularly sensitive to changes in the delivery of this benefit, especially where the change may involve an administrator other than Blue Cross/Blue Shield. There are several ways around this dilemma, including revision of contract language, better communication and education concerning the overall problem, and possibly making any significant changes in conjunction with the adoption of some sort of simplified flexible benefit program. Flexible benefits, besides providing considerable "sizzle" to a benefits program, can assist a municipality in capping costs.

Health Care Cost Containment in the Public Sector

James A. Landry

The rising cost of health care has caused employers in both public and private sectors to adopt a wide range of measures to manage and control medical benefit expenses. Public sector employers do not seem to be as aggressive as their counterparts in the private sector in using cost management techniques.

Mercer-Meidinger, in cooperation with the Public Risk and Insurance Management Association, surveyed 256 public employers across the United States, in May 1985. We asked them what they are now doing, or what they plan to do, to control medical costs.

What employers can do to manage health care costs

Strategies for managing healthcare costs fall into several categories:

1. Plan design—changing the balance of cost-sharing between employer and employee
2. Medical intervention—plan features which encourage employees to change the way they purchase medical care
3. Communications—educating and encouraging employees to become better consumers of health care
4. Preferred provider organizations—negotiating with health care providers and physicians for favorable rates
5. Health maintenance organizations—encouraging employees to enroll in prepaid health plans

---

Excerpted from *Healthcare Cost Containment in the Public Sector,* a Mercer-Meidinger Survey in cooperation with the Public Risk and Insurance Management Association, 1985.

6. Claims management—using data analysis of medical claims to identify potential problem areas
7. Claims administration—improving procedures so that improper claims are not paid
8. Lifestyle/wellness—programs to detect and prevent disease and encourage good health habits in employees.

We asked the respondents about their efforts in each of these areas.

Plan design

The most commonly used medical plan is basic medical/surgical plus major medical—which also tends to be the most generous kind of coverage, with the least cost-sharing by employees. In both public and private sectors, many employers are turning away from this kind of "first-dollar" coverage, although the private sector seems to be doing so more rapidly, according to several surveys by Mercer-Meidinger.

Basic medical/surgical plus major medical plans are offered by 52% of the surveyed agencies to their salaried employees, compared to only 38% of the private employers in our surveys.

For hourly employees, however, public sector and private sector still offer basic coverage at the same rate—45% of the employers. Since medical coverage is usually negotiated in union agreements, employers no doubt find it more difficult to replace basic coverage with less generous plans for their unionized employees.

Fewer than half of the public employers in the survey have adopted comprehensive plans, in which an employee co-payment is required for all or almost all medical services. In about half of the comprehensive plans, there is no first-dollar coverage, that is, employees must pay a portion of every medical expense. About one-quarter of the agencies have recently changed from basic to comprehensive plans, and another 15% said they are considering a change.

As shown in Figure 1, deductibles are $150 or less in 65% of the salaried plans, and 55% of the hourly plans—compared to 43% in the private sector.

About one-third of the agencies have more than one deductible. Half the responding agencies apply the deductible before hospital benefits are paid.

Other changes in plan design that the survey respondents said they have made or are considering:

1. Increasing maximum out-of-pocket limits—about 15% have changed, another 15% are considering. In 30% of the salaried plans and 26% of the hourly plans, the out-of-the-pocket limit is $500 or less; approximately the same percentages have $1,000 limits.

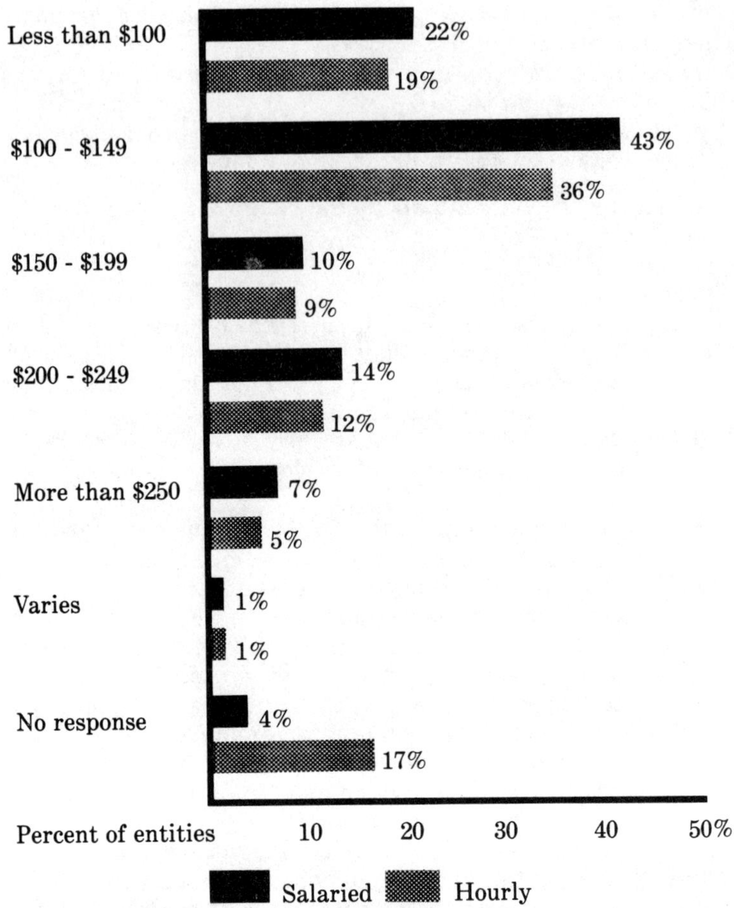

Figure 1. Deductibles in effect.

2. Increasing or adding employee contributions for medical coverage—about 12% have for employee coverage, almost 20% have for dependent coverage. About 21% are considering such changes.
3. Using a flexible spending account (IRS Section 125) for healthcare expenses—only 7% have actually made the change, but about 20% are considering.

Very few of the agencies have even considered other cost control changes such as increasing or adding contributions for short-service employees, or extending the waiting period before new employees are eligible for medical coverage.

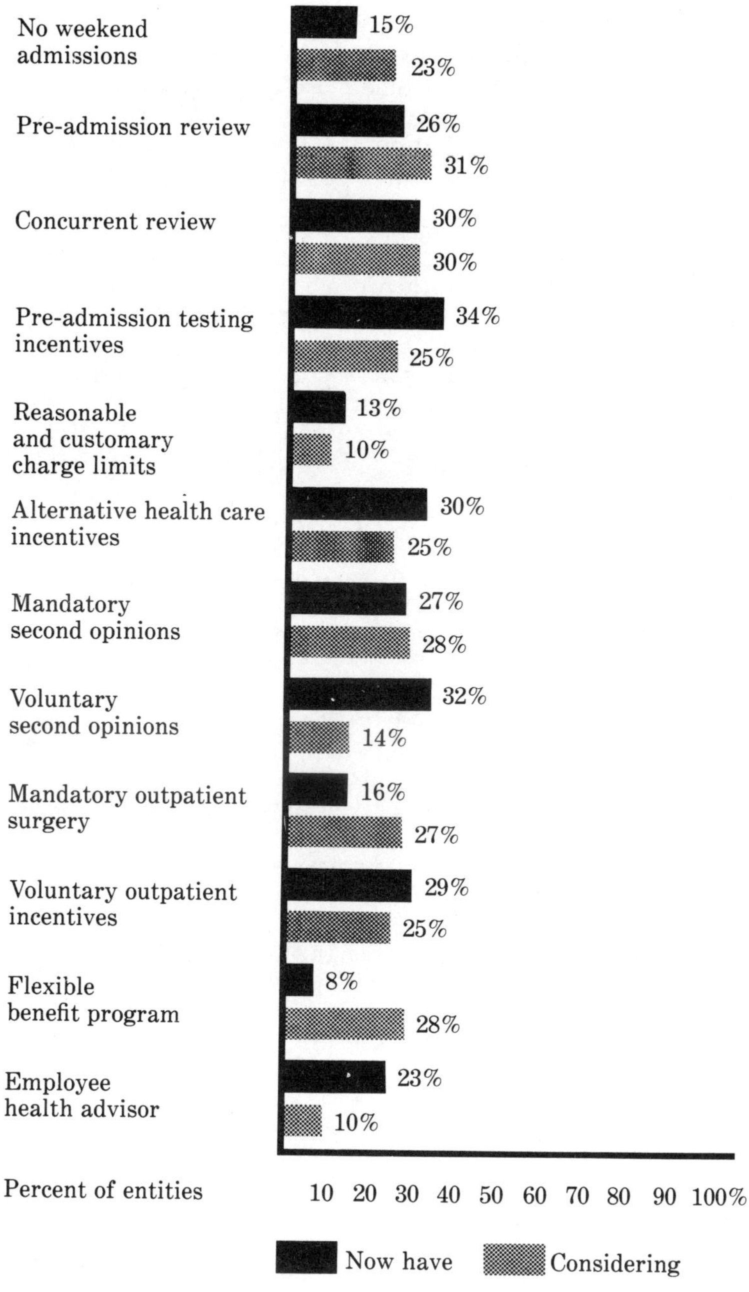

Figure 2. Cost-containment features in medical plans.

Medical intervention

As shown in Figure 2, employers have adopted a number of features which encourage employees to become more cost-conscious in using medical care. The most popular features are offering incentives for pre-admission testing and out-patient treatment, pre-admission review on elective admissions, and voluntary second surgical opinions.

Communication

The survey respondents said that employees' insulation from paying for health care was a major factor in escalating costs. Effective communications can be a way to break through this insulation and make employees aware of their part in controlling costs.

Thirty percent of the respondents said that a good communication program can have significant impact on helping reduce costs; another 55% said it can have a moderate impact. By contrast, employers in the private sector were much more likely to put their faith in communication.

About half of the agencies in the survey have put in special communication programs to deal with various aspects of health care—60% to introduce changes in benefit plans, 41% to enhance employees' understanding of their roles as purchasers, 53% to increase general health awareness, 50% for specific health education programs.

Preferred provider organizations

PPOs are multiplying across the United States as one way to control healthcare costs. These arrangements made between provider and employer usually offer discounted or negotiated fees in exchange for increased volume of patients.

According to the survey, public sector employers are ahead of their private-sector counterparts in offering PPOs—13% of the respondents, compared to about 3% in private-sector surveys. They seem receptive to offering such options in the future; 40% said they would offer a PPO from an "acceptable" provider; another 41% said they might. But potential savings would have to be significant to interest these agencies; only 30% said they would consider a PPO attractive if they thought they would save 11% or less.

The most important features of a PPO, according to the survey, are quality of providers, accessibility to employees, and discounts on service.

The most serious criticism of PPOs, according to the survey, was employee resistance to limited choice of provider (68% of the respondents). Other criticisms included the inability of employers to assess the quality of providers (29%) and the fact that 100% reimbursement for PPO services continues to insulate employees from the true costs of health care (28%).

Health maintenance organizations

More than half of the agencies—52%—offer HMO options to their employees, including 30% that offer more than one HMO. Since only 58% of the agencies have group practice HMOs available in their areas, and only 41% have individual practice association HMOs available, use of this service seems almost universal.

According to the survey, the most important feature in an HMO is the quality and number of hospitals and physicians available (69% of the respondents), with geographic location a distant second (42%). The respondents thought that the limited choice of providers would discourage employees from choosing HMOs.

The agencies who do not offer HMOs said that if they had the opportunity, they would anticipate that 5 to 15% of employees would enroll. These estimates may be low; of the agencies who do offer HMOs, the median enrollment rate is 27%.

Almost half of the survey respondents (44%) said they were interested in HMOs because they have the potential to reduce healthcare costs. However, 56% thought HMOs tend to siphon off younger, healthier employees, and as a result the costs of traditional plans will increase.

Claims management

Without detailed information on how benefit dollars are being spent, employers find it difficult to properly manage their medical costs. In response to the growing concern over healthcare costs, employers are asking their claims payers to provide this information, and insurance companies are responding with breakdowns of claims by disease category and other kinds of expenses.

While 59% of the agencies said the information provided by their claims payers was helpful in managing costs, only 35% have made any changes in their plans based on such information.

It may be that public sector employers are not getting the best information on which to make management decisions. Two-thirds said their claims reports are *not* compared to norms such as national, regional, local or industry. Only 22% receive summary data on inpatient and outpatient charges compared to total charges, and number of inpatient days and inpatient confinements per year per covered employee.

And only 27% of the respondents are using state-of-the-art data bases that use ICD-9-CM or CPT-4 five-digit coding. Not only do public sector employers seem slow to ask their carriers for sophisticated statistical data, 34% of the survey respondents said they were unfamiliar with such reports.

Asked what kind of information would be most helpful in managing costs, the survey respondents named reports identifying excessive or inappropriate utilization patterns (73%), excessive charges for medical procedures (67%) and specific hospital and provider cost figures (61%).

Claims administration

In 44% of the agencies, health plans are fully insured. Of those, 56% are fully experienced rated, and 35% pooled. Twenty-nine percent of the agencies have administrative services only arrangements, and 91% of those have stop-loss coverage.

Blue Cross/Blue Shield is used by 37% of the agencies, 25% use independent third-party administrators, 20% use commercial carriers, and 4% are self-administered. During the past two years 27% of the agencies have changed their administration arrangements.

Many of the public agencies use administrative techniques to limit or control claims, including coordination of benefits (89%), reimbursement according to reasonable and customary limits (85%), fixed dollar reimbursement schedules (41%) or audits of paid claims by the carrier or administrator (38%).

The carrier or administrator is responsible for verifying eligibility for claims payments in 76% of the agencies. Most of the administrators' claims systems (82%) are automated.

Lifestyle and wellness

Research has shown that people's lifestyles and health habits have a significant effect on their risk of disease, injury and death—and thus on their employers' medical costs. Yet employers tend to underestimate this effect. Almost half of the survey respondents (47%) thought employee lifestyle had only a moderate effect on medical costs, while 46% thought it has a significant effect. These opinions almost exactly match those of private sector employers in our surveys.

About one-fifth of the public sector respondents thought they could do little or nothing to change employees' lifestyles. More than one-half thought they could have a moderate effect, and only 15% thought they could have a significant effect. These responses could be colored by employers' recognition that monitoring these programs to ensure they are effective requires resources they often can't afford.

As shown in Figure 3, public employers are very interested in almost all types of lifestyle and wellness programs. But public sector employers are not taking the initiative in trying to improve lifestyles as much as their private sector counterparts. The most popular program named in public sector survey was alcohol and drug abuse—which is a reactive program, seeking to cure health problems rather than prevent them.

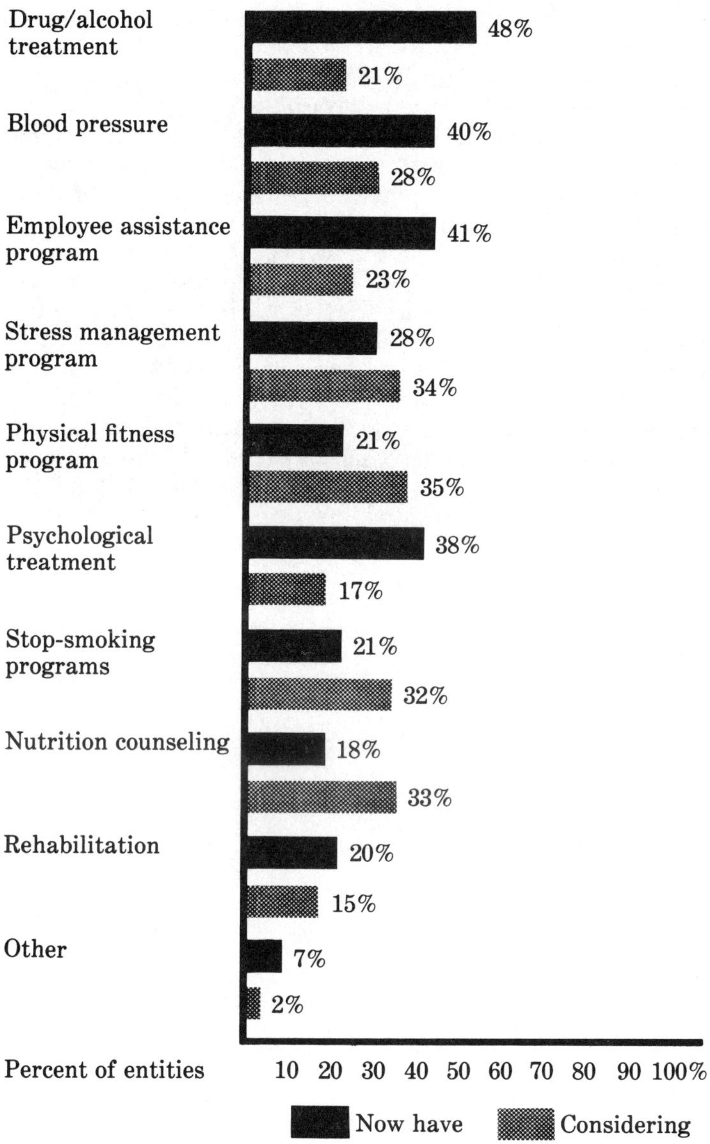

Figure 3. Features of wellness programs.

In conclusion

Asked which groups can and should act to bring healthcare costs under control, the agencies first named coalitions of employers and providers. Coalitions of employers ranked second. Tied for third were individual consumers acting in concert, and physicians. Unions ranked dead last.

Despite these opinions, only one-third of the agencies belong to any local employer cost containment group.

It would seem that public sector employers are slower to take action against rising healthcare costs than their private sector counterparts. They still provide relatively generous medical plans in which employees are insulated from the cost consequences of their decisions. They are not as aggressive in incorporating medical intervention features into their plans, or in adopting programs to prevent disease and encourage healthy lifestyles. They do not take full advantage of sophisticated data analysis techniques which can identify problem areas and thus lead to corrective measures. Finally, they are not active in local coalitions to control costs.

Employers are developing a wide variety of techniques to manage healthcare costs, and aggressive use of these techniques can deliver impressive bottom-line results. The public sector seems to be lagging in taking advantage of this knowledge.

A Blueprint for Controlling Workers Compensation Costs

Charles Woods

The purpose of this article is to assist municipal government in controlling workers compensation costs. This is not an easy task for two reasons. First, the continuing pressure of cost increases can be dealt with only partially at the local level since rates are established by state regulatory bodies. Second, most municipalities insure workers compensation through private insurance carriers, thereby effectively removing much of the cost control from the municipality. It is also likely that these costs will push ahead with continued inflation. This makes cost control a necessity for municipal government.[1]

A review

Workers compensation (WC) was first introduced in 1912 as a means of providing compensation to workers for accidents arising out of or during the course of employment. The laws have changed over the years to include occupational diseases which result from exposure to hazards in the work environment. Currently the law provides for four major types of benefits: temporary, temporary partial, permanent partial, and survivors death benefits. In addition, the concepts of blame and negligence were later eliminated and compensation is now paid without regard to fault.

Most employers (private or public) purchase insurance from an insurance carrier to fund workers compensation payments. Premiums are based on rates which are determined for each municipal job

Reprinted from *A Blueprint for Controlling Workers Compensation and Unemployment Insurance Costs,* prepared by the Illinois Department of Commerce and Community Affairs in 1981 through a grant from the U.S. Office of Personnel Management.

occupation. These manual rates are applied to the amount of municipal salaries in each category (i.e., police, firefighter, water plant operator) to determine base premium amount. A small but growing number of municipal employers have recently turned to alternative ways of funding compensation payments (i.e., self-insurance and cooperative self-insurance pools).[2]

Management experts estimate that on the average, municipalities expend anywhere from $30 to $50 additionally for every $100 of paid salary. This is not far-fetched when considering the customary assortment of indirect expenses associated with employees (i.e., pensions, health and life insurance, vacations, workers compensation, sick leave, unemployment insurance, and social security).

Workers compensation is one of these often hidden but always present indirect expenditures. It adds on the average 4 to 6 percent to the indirect costs borne by municipal employers. Unfortunately, most experts also feel this portion may grow as a result of a host of uncontrollable factors.

A municipality has but two opportunities to affect costs: the first comes prior to any accident, injury, layoff, and subsequent compensation claim. For discussion purposes, we refer to this opportunity as the *pre-incident* period.

The second critical opportunity is during and after the period when claims are made. This opportunity is referred to as the *post-incident* period. A municipality must be prepared to act at each of these important times if compensation costs are to be controlled. Techniques to utilize at both times follow.

Workers compensation cost control

Workers compensation costs are payroll based so, theoretically, the best way to control compensation costs is to systematically minimize the number of employees on the payroll or keep aggregate salary costs below an adjusted base year total. Keeping a lid on aggregate salary amounts is attractive on paper, but as we all know, this is easier said than done.

Another way to lower costs is to prevent compensable incidents from happening at all. This means preventing accidents and avoiding injuries.

A hardly desirable, although necessary, method of containment is to control for costs after an injury or accident occurs.

Pre-incident techniques, such as limiting salary costs[3] and preventing compensable incidents, generally have a much more favorable cost/benefit ratio than post-incident ones.

Pre-incident techniques There are two main sets of pre-incident cost control techniques. These are loss prevention techniques and workers compensation insurance management techniques.

Both will be reviewed in this section. One elementary but usually overlooked principle to keep in mind when considering workers compensation cost control through pre-incident techniques is simply: The more accidents, injuries, and claims a municipality has, the more workers compensation will cost.

Why is this principle so important? Municipalities engage in the provision of essential public services. They employ workers in a number of occupations including high risk ones such as police officers, firefighters, refuse collectors, and water or sewer plant operators. A number of job-related accidents will inevitably occur in the course of providing these sometimes hazardous services. After accidents and injuries come claims.

The key goal then is to work aggressively to reduce the number and severity of these accidents. Safety engineers and experts say that anywhere from 30 to 40 percent of all accidents are preventable. A major part of a loss prevention effort, then, will be a strong emphasis on on-the-job safety.[4]

A recent report concerning the overall lack of attention to loss prevention in the public sector indicates why this task is just now becoming so important.[5] Unfortunately, the same report indicates the serious absence of workers compensation loss prevention to date. A sampling of the report's highlights follows, as does a suggested approach to implementing a loss prevention program.

1. There is an immediate need for top management of public agencies and other employers to implement loss prevention policies. Loss prevention goals are virtually non-existent. Management has not expressed concern through a fixed policy statement and accountability is not fixed. Top management's lack of leadership impairs all other efforts to control workers compensation losses.
2. The lost time injury rate for nearly all job occupations is unacceptably high among local governments.
3. Either most agencies have not defined the scope of their own workers compensation problem, or no one is paying attention. There is a need for analysis of accidents and injuries so that corrective action can be taken to prevent them.
4. Efforts and legislation to date have been directed at less effective loss prevention measures in the physical surroundings of job sites. The majority of accidents are caused by unsafe acts, not unsafe conditions—it's a people problem. Loss prevention resources can be more effectively directed at people problems and then solved by management policies.
5. Safety education and training must be implemented and taken seriously. To reduce injury frequency, it will be necessary to create a safety *consciousness* throughout all public agencies.

6. A comprehensive approach to health control, especially for public safety officers, needs to be implemented.
7. There is a compelling need for communication on the workers compensation process with employees to ease their anxieties and establish claims management to reduce costs. Communication from the employer is often perceived by employees as substantially absent.
8. There is a need for greater medical control of workers compensation claims in public agencies.
9. There is also a need for a litigation avoidance effort by local agencies. Fifty percent of claims are a target for a litigation control effort.

How to implement a results oriented loss prevention program

Step one: Establish measurable goals First find out what the current lost-time, accident, or injury rate is for your entire municipality and for each department, if possible. The past three or five year picture is needed.

Existing record keeping practices may have been so lax that this information will have to be reconstructed from various files, insurance records and claims, and memories.

Once a rate is established, set a goal to reduce that rate by 20, 30, or 40 percent, etc., in the coming year.

Step two: Identify techniques and methods[6] Next, gather together as much written and verbal information on the various successful municipal loss prevention programs as possible. Contact safety engineering departments at universities, departments of labor, other municipalities, loss prevention engineers from existing insurance carriers, the Occupational Safety and Health Agency, and nearby industries for help.

Focus first on techniques to clean up unsafe conditions in the work environment. Then focus most of your efforts on unsafe acts or actions by current employees.

Arrive at a joint management/labor decision as to which techniques would be most effective in your municipality to lower injury rates. These should be based on the types of accidents, injuries, or claims previously experienced.

Step three: Assign responsibility Once useable techniques are defined, a municipality must assign responsibility for implementing the proposals.[7] Some prefer a safety committee with varying degrees of responsibility and authority, while other municipalities give the responsibility to each department. In any case, make sure the administrative apparatus selected has enough delegation of authority, resources, and legitimacy to do the job.

Step four: Devise timetable and implement strategy Formulate a timetable and an implementing strategy for the various techniques. Develop positive incentives and rewards (monetary or otherwise) for those individuals or departments that do well in avoiding injuries. Avoid penalties or disciplinary actions if possible. Finally, implement the techniques.

Step five: Monitor results Monitor the short and long term results of the loss prevention techniques. Pay close attention to the costs and expected benefits of the various methods. Continually refine, change, add to, or delete unproductive techniques when necessary. If accident and injury rates are reduced over the next two years, the claims and loss-ratios (claims paid over premiums paid) should begin to reflect the results.

Step six: Reduce costs Go to your insurance carrier or intergovernmental pool with the positive results in hand. If a favorable response in terms of a reduction in premium or a reduction in the rate of premium increases is not forthcoming, seek new competitive proposals.

The legitimate expectation of a premium reduction assumes, of course, that external developments have not intervened to raise manual rates, and that a municipality's employment and salary level has remained relatively constant. In fact, with a low injury rating, a municipality would be wise to seek competitive quotes every three years, especially if the rates are continually kept in check. The insurance markets constantly change and municipalities with low loss rates are in the best position to take advantage of the changes.

The eventual payback for a municipality that successfully implements a loss prevention program comes in many ways, including credits or premium rate adjustments from retrospective rating plans, lower in-house legal costs, improved productivity, improved ability to secure competitive quotes, lower claims costs in the case of self or pooled funded municipalities, improved employee morale, and a contribution to lower statewide costs.

Loss prevention is more than a safety program. Though a majority of accidents or injuries result because of the unsafe acts of individuals, there are other elements to loss prevention as well. A sizeable sampling of these follows:

1. Incorporate safety considerations into specifications of equipment purchases.
2. Provide and require the use of available safety equipment and gear (hard hats, steel toed shoes, bullet proof vests, gas detection devices, respiratory breathing devices, etc.).
3. Institute a voluntary or mandatory physical fitness program.

4. Develop adequate, realistic, and job-related medical standards.
5. Utilize agility screening for public safety officers.
6. Consider weight control contests.
7. Utilize anti-smoking, alcohol, and drug abuse campaigns.
8. Offer financial and other incentives for employees who demonstrate good safety records.
9. Post emergency phone numbers, procedures, and hospital locations in prominent places at work sites.
10. Train supervisors and employees in first aid, CPR, and other life-support procedures.
11. Train employees on the correct ways of performing various tasks.
12. Develop and institute an accident reporting system.
13. Develop and institute safety task forces and an accident review committee.
14. Hold supervisors accountable for accidents or injuries.
15. Adopt a municipal policy in regard to loss prevention.
16. Publish the workers compensation program benefits and process.
17. Conduct annual hazard surveys of all work sites.
18. Review all buildings and facilities for injury-producing design flaws.
19. Bring in available safety engineers from current insurance carriers.
20. Invite OSHA inspectors to perform a voluntary inspection of work sites.
21. Review all insurance policies, their costs, and coverages.
22. Restructure unsafe or hazardous work procedures.
23. Institute defensive driving training for all employees who operate vehicles.
24. Institute a litigation review process for future compensation claims through the municipal attorney.
25. Post notice of adequate insurance or self-insurance in a conspicuous place as well as information on the insurance carrier (or service company) such as address, policy number, effective date, etc.

From this list of pre-incident techniques, we want to elaborate on three of the most important ones; *pre-accident employee communications, pre-accident record keeping,* and finally, *workers compensation insurance management.* Communications, record keeping and insurance management form the key administrative factors to successful cost control.

Pre-incident employees communications The results of a survey of employees injured in work-related incidents indicate the importance of written and verbal communication prior to incidents. Most injured employees stated they were never aware of the existence of workers compensation benefits (e.g., what their rights and benefits are if they were injured).[8] What employees did know often came second-hand from fellow employees.

Out of fear of being "messed-over" through a lack of information, injured employees often turned immediately to outside legal help to protect their interests. Statistically, costs soar when legal assistance is sought. Unfortunately, as the Tannebaum report indicates, the only thing that employers communicate to counter this lack of information is "you will hear from our insurance company."[9]

Effective written and verbal communications on the workers compensation process—contrary to intuitive feelings to hide information—may go a long way in reducing ultimate claims and compensation costs. Essential pre-incident communications include:

1. Printing and distribution of information concerning the mechanics of various on-the-job injuries and the workers compensation program (for all employees).
2. Broad participation in formulation, creation, and operation of safety and accident review committees.
3. Selective use of visual media tools such as safety posters, brochures, payroll enclosures, etc.
4. Utilization of effective loss prevention training programs, and most importantly, the explanation of their importance to employees. Training should be periodic and feature the procedural and safety aspects of on-the-job responsibilities.
5. Reports on the findings of accident review committees.

Pre-incident record keeping A municipality would also be well advised to not attempt compensation cost control without a willingness and capacity to keep adequate records on relevant data. Accurate and accountable record keeping is a must. Without it, costs are not readily controllable.

There are numerous elements to an adequate records system. At a minimum, the records must:[10]

1. Form an effective accident reporting system. This must be a detailed form that records the facts from accidents and injuries requiring medical attention and time off from work.
2. Identify the principal sources of previous accidents by determining the material, machines, and tools most frequently involved in accidents, and the tasks most likely to produce injuries.
3. Disclose the nature and size of the accident problem within departments and occupations.

4. Isolate costs by department, division, and supervisor, thereby establishing accountability.
5. Provide cost information regarding injuries and accidents which will assist loss prevention minded personnel in spending their time in the most efficient manner.
6. Provide data for analysis of accidents and illnesses that point to specific causes which can then be controlled by specific counter-measures.
7. Disclose inappropriate job assignments where inabilities or physical handicaps contribute to accidents.
8. Provide supervisors, division, and department managers with hard facts about their safety problems so that their efforts can be concentrated.
9. Measure the effectiveness of individual counter-measures, and determine if specific programs are doing the job they were designed to do.

The fundamental record necessary to accomplish these purposes is, of course, the accident report form. Accurate completion of this form must be within 24 to 48 hours of an accident. When accident reports are received, they form a basis for the analysis and review functions. They also provide documentation for the post-incident review process. Other important records include individual employee medical histories, health control data (i.e., physical examination tickler files which generate lists of employees due for physicals: 21 to 29 years of age every 3 years, 30 to 39 every 2 years, and 40 and over every year), and a legal review statement on all accident reports to assess potential liability.

Pre-incident insurance management This section applies to those municipalities who insure their workers compensation expenditures through insurance companies. Regardless of how your municipality secures its current coverage (e.g., assigned risk pool, competitive proposals or allocations, historical use of one carrier), several cost control techniques can be readily utilized.

The company that provides workers compensation coverage determines a municipality's basic premium by first recording the number of employees employed in various municipal job classifications (e.g., police officer, firefighter, sewage disposal worker, etc.). The amount of salary paid in these various occupations forms the initial premium amount when applied to a "manual rate" established for each classification. The rate for police officers, for instance, is less than that for firefighters based on historical claims data. The product of this aggregate salary amount multiplied by the manual rate is then usually adjusted by a year-end audit, and later refined to reflect any applicable experience modifier.

One useful technique in this area is to recheck the number of employees the insurance company has listed for each classification. Remember, certain classifications have rates more expensive than others. An employee who is incorrectly posted as a waterline laborer ($6.85 per $100 of salary) is inherently more expensive than the correct category of street cleaner ($4.94 per $100 of salary).

Another cost control technique is to make sure your employees are placed in categories based on legitimate work assignments. If an employee is a streets cleaner who spends one day a year with the water department or sewer crews, he/she should not be listed in the latter classifications.

Other techniques include: (1) removal of manual rate applications to salary which was paid but work not actually performed (vacation time, sick leave, etc.); and (2) removal of manual rate applications to aggregate salaries that are exaggerated by overtime payrates (time and a half).

A great deal of fluctuation has occurred in the municipal insurance market over the last few years. Yet many cities and villages remain relatively stable when it comes to claims history. This group of municipalities still have an opportunity to secure competitive proposals for workers compensation coverage.

Most experts feel requests for proposals on insurance coverage should be made not less than every three to five years. If the claims experience ratio in your municipality has been consistently stable, it would be in the best interests of your taxpayers to at least test the competitive market. Long standing but not necessarily competitive carriers can deal a blow to compensation cost control.

Post-incident techniques Thus far the focus has been on techniques and methods to cut costs before an incident or potentially compensable incident. In the pre-incident section, the techniques were geared towards preventing incidents (accidents, injuries, or terminations, etc.) which would contribute greatly to higher compensation costs. Our assumption is that a strong commitment by municipal management *prior* to an incident could save money. Now the attention shifts to those techniques during or after an incident.

Post-incident techniques constitute the second and last opportunity to control compensation costs. It's the damage control phase of compensation cost-control. When a worker is injured, the foremost goal is to assure prompt, skilled, and top-notch medical care. Once this is assured, the emphasis needs to revert to managerial cost control techniques.

Many municipalities are essentially unprepared when an accident or injury happens. Unfortunately, the critical moments just after an accident often determine if a simple claim will develop into a more serious disability claim.

Each and every time an accident happens, the immediate work supervisor must be prepared to take prompt and correct action.

They must be trained and knowledgeable in assessing the nature and severity of any injury. Proper on-site first aid, CPR, or other life sustaining techniques must be known and utilized by both employees and supervisors when necessary.

The implementation of practiced emergency procedures must be activated almost automatically to govern actions such as emergency transportation, hospital destination, and applicable emergency medical information. Only after professional medical help is secured can the task of reporting the accident and investigating the events leading up to the accident take place.

Remember, assuring prompt and immediate medical attention is the municipality's first and only priority until the injured worker is transferred to skilled medical care. Workers who are scurrying about in panic or arguing about "whose fault the accident was" create a potentially dangerous situation. Training, printed information, periodic drills, and well publicized emergency procedures are a must for injured worker care regardless of the severity of anticipated injuries. Municipalities choosing to ignore this advice may well find themselves contributing to the filing of trauma claims.

The multitude of cost-control activities must be sorted our prior to an incident of the limited amount of time and resources any municipality can devote to workers compensation cost control. It will help to plan a cost control program if injuries are grouped into categories of lower to higher severity:[11]

1. Minor injuries. When combined they constitute a numerical majority of reported claims and a significant portion of total claim expenditures. These cause no loss of time.
2. Minor temporary disability injuries. Composed principally of soft tissue injuries and simple fractures that may require some loss of work time.
3. Serious temporary disability injuries. These injuries are serious enough to cause temporary disabling conditions and usually require treatment by specialists. These can evolve into more serious permanent disabling injuries if not properly handled.
4. Permanent partial disability injuries. Includes heart attacks, spinal injuries, cumulative trauma cases, etc. These severe injuries will result in the injured party receiving permanent disability after the injury heals.

These categories can help in determining where a municipality's efforts will be initiated. Over a period of time the arsenal of utilized techniques should become all inclusive, and minor injuries and permanent disability injuries should be treated with equal dispatch although with varying degrees of intensity.

After the injured party has received necessary medical attention, the municipality must turn its attention to post-incident techniques These techniques *do not* include depriving injured workers of legitimate medical, surgical, and hospital services as well as necessary physical, mental, and vocational rehabilitation and disability pay. These must be provided regardless of who was at fault.

The municipality must instead focus on ensuring that these expenditures are kept within the benefits provided by law. Second, a municipality must work to avoid any or all litigation which stems from an injury or death.

Contact injured worker Begin by initiating immediate contact, if possible, with the injured worker. Work to remove fears about medical bills, temporary income compensation, job security, etc. Contact the injured employee's family to aid in their needs at this critical time. Discuss the condition and progress of the injured worker with the attending physicians.

Monitor claims costs The first action to take is to obtain relevant information that may be needed for subsequent claims investigations. Establish a workers compensation case file[12] which will eventually contain information such as:

1. Employee's name, address, phone, name of spouse or relative
2. Department, occupation/job classification
3. Age, date hired
4. Date and time of injury, including hour of day and hour of shift, date injury was reported, and to whom
5. Accident report form
6. Other descriptions of accident (be specific)
7. Location of accident
8. Witnesses, name, address, position
9. Nature and extent of injury, part of body, disability rating
10. Object/substance causing injury
11. Name and address of treating physician(s), treatment to date, estimated future treatment, hospital, ambulance, X-rays
12. Third party, name, address, phone, insurance, lawyer
13. Police report
14. Applicant's attorney, name, address, phone
15. Contractors, defense attorney, sub rosa investigator, etc.
16. Reserve or estimated cost of claim
17. Reciprocal benefits claimed (i.e., disability retirement health, and accident policies, group insurance benefits);
18. Past history: operations, accidents, periods of disability, and previous compensation benefits received.

Keep in mind that workers compensation carriers pay two types of benefits—medical and disability. A municipality would be wise to scrutinize both aspects of claims expense. Insist upon a partnership with your carrier in monitoring and questioning unnecessary or incorrect bills from hospitals, physicians, etc. Require that insurance carriers provide prompt listings of claims paid as per Illinois law.[13]

Don't assume your carrier conducts a tight review of the bills submitted. Many carriers do not have, for example, standards or fee guidelines to compare with bills. Refuse to participate in claims that are not legitimate. Urge your carrier to appeal decisions and claims that are not valid because some carriers view their role almost passively as a bills processor for the municipality.[14]

This makes it imperative to closely watch all bills paid. If necessary, seek second medical opinions or independent verification of hospital and clinical costs paid by your carrier. Raise objections to the insurance carrier (or service company) if, in your view, an unjustified bill has been paid.

Avoid litigation One of the ultimate objectives of cost-control activities is to avoid a legal dispute. Good claims management which features aggressive pre- and post-incident communication with injured employees works hand-in-hand with avoiding long and expensive legal cases. Retaining legal expertise knowledgeable in the workers compensation area may be helpful in avoiding litigation. Settlements should be sought to avoid expensive litigation but they must be fair, equitable, and minimize the risk of a reopened claim. If the case reaches a point where an unjustified settlement is rendered, then the appeals process is available to the municipality.[15] Ensure that the municipal management team makes these critical decisions and not disinterested insurance carriers or legal advisors.

Analyze incidents Beginning with the completion of an accident report form, there must be prompt and complete review of all conditions and actions surrounding the incident. Prompt and effective follow-up may be immediately required to prevent similar incidents from occurring.

This is where the various elements of a pre-incident program interchange with post-incident techniques and are adjusted if necessary. Remember to commend those who reacted correctly during and after the incident in a positive way. Information obtained throughout the process from the time of injury to the closing of the case, should be used and not ignored in future loss prevention efforts. Other specific techniques to utilize while contacting injured workers, monitoring claims costs, avoiding litigation, and analyzing incidents are listed below:

1. Print and disseminate information on post-injury procedures.
2. Maintain and post the names of physicians, osteopaths, surgeons, and hospitals which are certified and acceptable to the municipality.

3. Distribute descriptions of applicable state legislation.
4. Remind employees in writing of the responsibility to notify employees of any work connected injury or disability as the result of occupational disease.
5. Request that injured employees inform the municipality in writing of their decision to seek medical services from those originally providing services.
6. Demand the best possible medical treatment for injured workers including specialists if necessary.
7. Avoid unnecessary forensic opinions that add to costs without contributing to treatment.
8. Monitor hospital and clinic costs regarding visits, frequency of X-rays, drugs, and other services.
9. Insist upon annual claims reports from carriers.
10. Insist that insurance carriers furnish proof of having reasonable fee structures based on acceptable medical treatment standards.
11. Monitor minor and temporary disability injuries to prevent them from developing into extended temporary or permanent injuries.
12. Resist claims or object to the payment to such claims if clear medical or legal justification exists to do so.
13. Secure all reports within 24 to 48 hours of the accident.
14. Develop a post-injury sequence of events or a checklist to govern necessary actions following an injury (i.e., follow-up phone calls, physician contacts, legal review).
15. Develop an in-house procedure to have direct and ongoing communications with injured employees and their families.
16. Establish communications with every doctor treating the injured employee.
17. Encourage the workers compensation carrier to have a viable rehabilitation manual on hand with specific criteria to assist in the readjustment of injured employees into the work environment.
18. Become aware of disability standards which govern when an injured employee can return to work.
19. Assist directly in return to work efforts by offering encouragement, assistance, and modified work assignments.
20. Become aware of the facts concerning vocational rehabilitation in lieu of disability retirement.
21. Retain only legal firms experienced in workers compensation to represent the municipality's interest.
22. Prepare information concerning all circumstances surrounding a claim applicant's job activities, attitudes, medical history, medical and legal reports from the applicant's attorney (for rebuttal), X-rays, and other pertinent information for

presentation to the arbitrator, industrial commission, or court of law.

23. Seek agreements with litigant or applicant attorneys on mutually acceptable medical examiners for disability evaluation purposes.
24. Contract with professional investigators to check into the facts of the claim prior to accepting or rejecting a very serious accident claim.
25. Prepare to assist the workers compensation carriers if a case reaches arbitration stage.
26. Consider subrogation as a means to recover claims costs as a result of negligence caused by a third party (not including co-employees).

Summary

Active consideration of a number of these widely accepted techniques (pre- and post-incident) will assist in controlling workers compensation costs. Many of the most successful techniques that a municipality can utilize in devising their own cost control blueprint are complex while some are rather simple. Preventing all too likely cost increases calls for the utilization of any and all available methods.

1. Background information for the content of this publication was obtained from a publication entitled *Managing Workers Compensation,* Institute for Local Self Government, Hotel Claremont Building, Berkeley, California 94705, 1979.
2. The techniques described in this publication are generally applicable to municipalities who are conventionally insured via insurance companies, as well as those who are self-insured.
3. Detailed information on keeping salary costs at a minimum are discussed in the Cost-Cutter monograph, *Cost Reduction Through Better Workforce Utilization.*
4. Loss prevention is defined as a combination of safety, accident prevention, claims management, and other policies designed to minimize the number of claims, losses, and costs.
5. *Equity Eroded,* Institute for Local Self-Government (Berkeley, California, 1977).
6. A sample list of pre-incident techniques follows this step-by-step presentation. Be advised that each and every technique is currently being utilized successfully by some municipality somewhere in the country.
7. *Cutting Costs With a Safety Program* (Institute of Government, Terrell Hall, Athens, Georgia, 1977).
8. The Illinois Department of Insurance also confirmed this finding through a report entitled *Workers Compensation: A Blueprint for Cost Containment* published in 1980, pages 9-11. The report is commonly referred to as the "Tannebaum Report" after its hearing officer.
9. Ibid, page 16.
10. *Managing Workers Compensation,* page 79.
11. Ibid., page 171.
12. Ibid., page 142.
13. Effective January, 1981.
14. Tannebaum Report, page 18.
15. *Summary of Illinois Workers Compensation Act and Illinois Occupational Disease Act* (Illinois Industrial Commission, 160 North LaSalle St., Chicago, IL 60601) and *Ready Reference on Illinois Workers Compensation* (Illinois State Chamber of Commerce, 20 North Wacker Drive, Chicago, IL 60606).

PART 5

Conclusion

Case Studies in Risk Management

In the past several years, governments have found risk management programs to be very beneficial. In January 1985, a request in *Public Management* magazine generated a flood of responses from administrative personnel and local government managers as to the value of risk management. Some of the benefits they cited include:

1. Reduces or stabilizes insurance costs
2. Improves internal communication through coordination and centralization of records
3. Emphasizes the management of claims to control and/or reduce loss
4. Promotes safety awareness and training resulting in cost savings and reduction in injuries
5. Stresses the importance of the employee's health and well-being
6. Identifies those exposures that should be insured and seeks adequate coverage or retention for them.

Some of the responses received from that survey are reprinted below.

Wichita Falls, Texas

What can a risk manager do for you that's not already being done by your city attorney or finance director? Save you money, that's what.

The city of Wichita Falls has employed a risk manager for

Reprinted with permission from the February and March 1985 issues of *Public Management* magazine, published by the International City Management Association.

nearly eight years. Under the direction of Mark Wilson, our risk manager, we have:

1. Averaged a $200,000 annual savings on our workers compensation program by going self-insured.
2. Reduced our fleet liability insurance from $123,000 in FY 80-81 to $31,933 in FY 83-84.
3. Reduced our overall insurance premiums from $325,000 in FY 79-80 to $204,000 in FY 84-85.
4. At the same time, we have improved our insurance coverages by adding public official, police professional, medical clinics, and general liability policies.

All of this was accomplished through careful analysis of the available insurance products and an evaluation of what level of risk the city could afford to undertake on its own. For example, we are saving close to $100,000 per year on our fleet liability policy through changing from coverage at $25,000 per person, $50,000 per occurrence, $10,000 property damage to a $10 million combined single limit policy with a $100,000 self-insured retention.

By changing most of our coverages to accept a higher level of risk, we are not only saving money but have an incentive to pursue aggressive safety and loss control programs. Our vehicle operators must complete periodic in-house defensive driving courses; all vehicle and industrial accidents are reviewed and investigated; city-wide safety manuals have been prepared and are supplemented by divisional manuals dealing with specific safety problems.

In addition, risk management deals personally and frequently with all employees who are unable to work due to industrial accidents. This contact ensures that our employees are receiving the medical care they need and maintains their ties with us. The result: Injured employees return to work much sooner than in the past, since employer concern and contact are maintained.

Oh, by the way, our general liability claims paid rarely exceed $15,000 per year for a city of 100,000.

We save $300,000 to $500,000 a year by funding a risk management division. Our cost is about $80,000 per year. On the side, our risk manager also serves as our defense coordinator and handles the subrogation of our claims against others.

Can you afford a risk manager? Maybe the real question is: Can you afford not to have a risk manager?

—Edward A. Barrett, Assistant City Manager, and James Berzina, City Manager

Chino, California

Prior to July 1981, there was no centralized risk management function in the city of Chino. The personnel department, finance department, and the safety officer, who reported to the director of community development, each was responsible for various aspects of risk management without formal organizational pressures for coordination and cooperation between the three. As a result, the city's workers compensation and general liability administrators found it difficult to obtain needed information for evaluation of claims, which in turn hampered the city's ability to prepare an adequate defense.

In July, 1981, the city council restructured the departmental organization and incorporated a centralized risk management function with administrative responsibility under the personnel department. Over the past four years, this centralized administration of risk management has provided a number of benefits for the city:

1. Centralized preparation/coordination for the defense of claims
2. Single person responsible to ensure proper administration of claims
3. Cost savings through innovative safety programs, proper administration, and follow-up of claims
4. Improved internal communication/coördination
5. Ability to provide directed safety and other cost savings programs to employees
6. Ensuring the city is properly covered for its various exposures.

Overall, centralization of the risk management function in the city of Chino has proven to be extremely beneficial from both cost, and administrative standpoints.

—Jim Hart, Director of Personnel and Risk Management

Hampton, Virginia

The city of Hampton is a coastal community encompassing 57 square miles in southeastern Virginia, with a population of 125,000.

In November 1977, alarmed by increasing costs of commercial insurance, a lack of available coverage for some municipal needs, and an unsatisfactory accident history, city officials established a risk management department.

The initial task of this new department was to stem the accident rate, to identify hazards and exposures common to most municipalities, and to provide insurance coverage as economically as possible for those losses that could not be controlled. This was accomplished over time by establishing a self-insurance fund for workers compensation, by introducing substantial deductibles for property and casualty programs, by managing a majority of claims in-house, and, most of all, through the establishment of an employee safety program.

Hampton's risk management program has produced dollar savings. Since 1978, insurance savings have totally funded the risk management department and still generated savings in excess of $200,000 annually. A "common sense driving course," which provides driver training to all vehicle operators, has been implemented. This program is recognized as second to none in the state of Virginia, and details are regularly requested from other safety divisions. Today, risk management is no longer limited to safety and insurance management; it is viewed as an opportunity to improve operations throughout the city in a manner that benefits both citizens and employees. Over the past two years, as the cost savings became evident, the city's program grew to encompass school operations and regional academies located in Hampton. The school board now self-insures its workers compensation program, with the city's risk management department providing management control and claims service; as a result, cost savings have averaged more than $30,000 per year. Additionally, the city conducts semiannual safety inspections of all school and play areas; cooperation from the schools in correcting safety deficiencies has been outstanding.

In support of the regional police and fire academies, safety courses in defensive and pursuit driving are provided to all police and fire personnel. In addition to savings from fewer accidents, this program reduces the overhead cost of these institutions, which in turn reduces the necessary contributions from each locality in the region.

As previously indicated, our programs are designed to provide benefits that, in addition to our saving money, contribute to the community as well. By focusing our attention on programs that increase efficiency and employee performance, we improve service delivery to our citizens, which in turn enhances the quality of life throughout the city of Hampton, Virginia.

—Patrick A. Hanrahan, Risk Management Officer

Longmont, Colorado

The city of Longmont is a full-service city with 47,000 citizens and nearly 530 full-time employees. Services provided by the city cover the full range of municipal activities from water, sewer, and electric utilities to sanitation, fire, and parks and recreation. It also has much in common with public entities across this nation, including the continuing erosion of governmental immunity and broadening responsibilities under modern workers compensation statutes. Until 1970, however, the city had no specific strategy for dealing with these loss-producing concerns, and the problems in this area grew larger.

In January of 1970, the city of Longmont created a new job classification—city safety officer. The emphasis of this new position was to create a program that would help management promote safety awareness on the job and provide some safety training for city employees, such as first aid and CPR. This initial step, having broken new ground with some measure of success, led to the creation of the city's risk management office in the spring of 1978. Under this more formalized approach to tackling safety and liability concerns, the risk management office, under the direction of a risk manager, divided its energies into three major areas of responsibility.

1. Loss prevention: Working to prevent a negative occurrence.
2. Loss control: Claims management and investigation aimed at reducing or controlling the loss once something negative has occurred.
3. Loss financing: Planning for insurance coverages and self-insured retentions to meet loss-financing needs.

When compared with the rising tide of public entity litigation and rapidly increasing costs for workers compensation coverages, the city's risk management program has produced results it can be proud of.

1. Between 1979 and 1984, employee injury losses have been reduced from a high of nearly $230,000 per year to less than $74,000 in 1983, and only $35,000 in the first three-quarters of 1984.
2. Workers compensation experience modification rating has changed in the same time period from a high of 1.55 to a low of 1.08.
3. Property/casualty insurance premiums from 1979 through 1985 have remained relatively constant, while public entity risks and insurer exposures have increased dramatically during the same time period.
4. With the exception of one bad year, total dollars paid toward claims against the city between 1979 and 1984 have been reduced nearly 50 percent.

Today, the city's risk management office is staffed with a full-time risk manager and risk management technician. This office processes, investigates, and maintains records on all property, liability, and workers compensation claims. They also follow up on problem calls from the public, reducing liability exposures. They provide first aid, CPR, and defensive driving classes for employees and more specific occupational safety and health training for individual divisions within the city.

This comprehensive, well-focused approach to risk management has allowed the city of Longmont to hold its own against the sleeping giant of uncertainty and the increasing responsibilities thrust upon today's public entities.

—Geoff Dolan, Assistant City Manager, and Peter Potemkin, Risk Management Officer

Fort Worth, Texas

The city of Fort Worth maintains a risk management division within the personnel department with the full support of city management. Looking at the forefront of its success, this division is a key tool for top management since it provides direction for their cost-beneficial and resource-reserving decisions.

The structure of the risk management division includes administration of the following programs that can greatly affect the financial integrity of the city: workers compensation, safety, health benefits, property and casual insurance, and third-party claims, which includes an aggressive approach to subrogation. Perhaps one of the unique aspects of the organization is that it includes a claims adjuster to handle all third-party claims and subrogation. The division continues involvement, with coordination with the department of law, when claims become litigious.

Paramount to the organization's risk management is the identifying of loss exposures, which are analyzed on frequency and severity bases. The treatment of risks continues, but this is reevaluated when a risk changes or when the costs of the risks change.

An integral part of risk management's operations is the active communication network maintained with all city departments. For instance, exposure survey information and departmental inquiries on risks are received and responded to with practical programs, procedures, and guidelines.

Due to this communication, risks are prevented or eliminated. For example, a waterslide was not purchased to embellish the park and recreation program. Also, risks can be transferred. For instance, fire and extended coverage insurance on city buildings and contents protects against catastrophic losses over a $100,000 self-insured retention. Moreover, risks are assumed. For example, general liability insurance covering certain city premises was not renewed when the premise cost would have quadrupled. Considering this, managers of the facilities that were once covered worked closely with risk management to reduce exposures to bodily injuries to third parties. In addition, risks are reduced. For instance, a practical employee safety program is in force to help keep the number of "first aids" and workers compensation cases down. Finally, catastrophic and stop-loss commercial insurance has been obtained to limit loss to the city.

It needs to be pointed out that treating loss exposures usually involves a carefully determined combination of the methods mentioned, as well as considering the cost-benefit factors.

"Due to changes in legislation and court judgments, public entities no longer enjoy the luxury of governmental immunity in areas where $300,000 was the limit of liability loss," stated Bill Herrington, risk manager, city of Fort Worth. Moreover, "As more public services require user fees, the proprietary aspect of many city functions has propelled us into the arena of unlimited liability, necessitating a well-supported and importantly recognized risk management program such as the city of Fort Worth carries out," Herrington added.

In conclusion, the city of Fort Worth's risk management needs have been well defined. These staff members' efforts have been a tremendous asset to the city's top management.

—Susan Williams, Administrative Analyst

Johnson County, Kansas

Johnson County, Kansas, is an urban county of 382,000 near Kansas City, Missouri. The county began efforts to manage its risk and insurance in 1980 with the addition of an insurance coordinator to the finance department.

Staff efforts were directed toward improving the county's insurance program from the standpoint of cost, coverage, and administration. Competitive bidding was implemented, and various individual department policies were consolidated. Improved loss control procedures and claims administration controls were also instituted.

In many cases, the results were dramatic. In 1981-82, automobile insurance premiums dropped nearly $20,000, while the number of autos insured went up by 90. By consolidating six individual policies and increasing deductibles, property insurance premiums decreased $40,000, while at the same time property values were updated to reflect current replacement costs. Workers compensation claims were reduced $12,000 compared with the average of the four years prior to beginning the program, and the county's experience modification factor has dropped every year since. In addition, closer audits of premium returns, adjusted losses, and similar contractual responsibilities of the insurance companies resulted in $9,800 of returned premium from the county's workers compensation carrier. Blue Cross and Blue Shield returned more than $60,000 due to adjusted losses' falling below paid premiums on the county's cost-plus contract. And, finally, paying attention to premium payment options on consolidated policies resulted in improved cash flow, which increased investment income to the county by approximately $17,000 in both fiscal years 1981 and 1982.

In 1983, the county began an innovative flexible benefit plan for its employees. Under the plan, the county contributes a certain amount each month on behalf of each full-time employee. Employees may allocate the contribution among several health and dental insurance plans, to deferred compensation, or to a "medical reimbursement bank" managed by a third-party administrator. Employees may use medical reimbursement bank funds on a reimbursement basis for any legitimate health expenses that are tax deductible, including treatment, private insurance premiums, or to satisfy insurance deductibles. In addition to being more equitable for county employees, the flexible benefit plan also gives the county increased control of its future benefits costs. In 1984, the National Association of Counties gave Johnson County an award for its innovative plan.

In 1984, the finance department took additional steps to improve the county's risk and insurance management. Outside risk management consultants recommended increased limits of liability in several areas, as well as some further consolidation of coverages. Based on the consultants' recommendations, an RFP was prepared for combined bids on property, liability (excluding automobile liability), and aviation insurance (the county's airport commission operates two airports). The bids received indicate that the premium increases expected from increasing limits of liability will be offset by the effects of combining coverages, so that overall costs will go up only slightly. As an example, in one instance it will be possible to replace separate policies costing $14,000 by a $500 rider to a consolidated policy!

In the future, the insurance coordinator will concentrate on improving the organization of the county's manual claims records. An automated data base will be developed to allow easier identification and statistical analysis of loss experience by department, type of loss, and other variables. With this information, it will be possible to begin to determine with more certainty the county's major exposures and hazards. This will make it possible to implement a more active loss control program to protect property and minimize legal exposure to employees and the public, thus leading to additional cost reduction. Up to now, analysis of claims and other records has been difficult due to the lack of automated records. And keeping in mind that any insurance coverages required of vendors and contractors will affect costs to the county, the office will also review insurance requirements on contracts and RFPs to ensure that coverages requested are adequate but not excessive.

Johnson County's 1985 budget for insurance premiums, including workers compensation but not health, life, and dental insurance, was nearly $600,000. The overhead cost of the risk management operation have been minimal. The 1985 budget for the office was less than $40,000. Based on the past savings generated and the importance of minimizing future exposure to loss, Johnson County feels that this expenditure continues to be a good investment in its fiscal integrity.

—Jack Manahan, Assistant Director of Finance

Springfield, Ohio

Risk management in the city of Springfield has been a team effort on the part of the purchasing division of finance and the personnel department. The city's purchasing agent and safety and benefits specialist have probably paid their wages by their perseverance in saving the city money in insurance and safety measures.

Although this has been a good year in claims on health care insurance for the city, a close watch on prescriptions and health care claims by employees has reduced the expected 1984 expenditure of $1.7 million to $1.2 million. Going to a minimum premium coverage, monitoring utilization reports, and getting the employees involved in health care procedures and prevention programs have contributed to the difference.

Personnel from the two divisions work together on health care monitoring. This insurance is the biggest user of city dollars and must be studied carefully. Seeking advice from professionals in the field has made a big difference in expenditures, and using the shopping list of benefits available to its full advantage is necessary.

The safety and benefits specialist spends considerable time on workers compensation and unemployment compensation claims, as well as on monitoring health care claims. Getting employees involved in health awareness programs is seen as a crucial step to reducing costs in claims and lost work hours.

This specialist also coordinates the city safety committee, comprised of representatives of the police, fire, and AFSCME unions, parks department, city fleet manager, and public properties manager. This committee investigates all accidents and injuries in the city organization and makes recommendations to city officials for improvements in operations and employee procedures.

The specialist does the usual safety training and inspects operations and personnel to ensure that personnel are adequately protected for the job and that unsafe working conditions are eliminated. He checks all work areas in the city periodically and does periodic inspections of vehicles for proper working conditions.

Risk management also includes the city of Springfield employee assistance program (EAP), which provides help for employees under stress or under the influence of chemicals. The EAP helps employees to be more productive while at work which, in turn, helps to reduce personal injury and vehicular accident rates. These employees are usually the heavy users of health care benefits (which also have been reduced through EAP).

Over the past few years, several necessary changes have been made in property insurance, such as insuring all properties under one blanket policy at replacement value. Seeking professional advice from consultants, arranging for self-funding, and using higher deductibles have made drastic differences in costs. Continual monitoring of all programs has saved the city more than 30 percent in costs. Several thousand dollars also were saved by eliminating some city-owned properties from the real estate tax rolls through reclassification.

Keeping good loss control records and centralizing insurance management have also made a difference. To be completed this year is the conversion of this information to the in-house computer. The city's good fire and fleet record is also important. The former is evidenced in the recent Class 2 rating for fire.

All of this information is plenty to keep track of, so early on in setting-up procedures an insurance risk committee was established within the city organization. The committee includes representatives from the city manager's office, finance, personnel, and the legal departments. The committee reviews policies and related activities, reviews specifications, and makes recommendations to the management.

Many of these procedures are common among businesses and many cities, although more cities should be more involved in the study of where money can be saved. Springfield keeps the risks low and thus has saved much money at a time when every dollar counts.

—Ann Armstrong, Information Coordinator

Practical Management Series

Risk Management Today:
A How-to Guide for Local Government

Text type
Century Expanded

Composition
Unicorn Graphics
Washington, D.C.

Printing and binding
R. R. Donnelley & Sons Company
Harrisonburg, Virginia

Cover design
Rebecca Geanaros